Scotland
MountainBiking
The Wild Trails

D1434598

VERTEBRATE **PUBLISHING**

Design and production by Vertebrate Publishing, Sheffield
www.**v-publishing**.co.uk

Scotland
MountainBiking
The Wild Trails

Written by
Phil McKane

Photography by **Andy McCandlish**

Scotland
MountainBiking
The Wild Trails

VG Copyright © 2009 Vertebrate Graphics Ltd and Phil McKane

VP Published by Vertebrate Publishing

All rights reserved. No part of this work covered by the copyright hereon may
be reproduced or used in any form or by any means – graphic, electronic, or
mechanised, including photocopying, recording, taping, or information storage
and retrieval systems – without the written permission of the publisher.

ISBN 978-1-906148-10-2

Cover photo: Al Byford in Glencoe.
Photography by **Andy McCandlish, unless otherwise credited.**

Design by Nathan Ryder. Production by Al Williams.
www.**v-publishing**.co.uk

VERTEBRATE **PUBLISHING**

Every effort has been made to achieve accuracy of information in this guidebook.
The authors, publishers and copyright owners can take no responsibility for: loss or
injury (including fatal) to persons; loss or damage to property or equipment; trespass,
irresponsible riding or any other mishap that may be suffered as a result of following
the route descriptions or advice offered in this guidebook. The inclusion of a track or path
as part of a route, or otherwise recommended, in this guidebook does not guarantee that
the track or path will remain a Right of Way. If conflict with landowners arises we advise
that you act politely and leave by the shortest route available. If the matter needs to be
taken further then please take it up with the relevant authority.

PLEASE GIVE WAY TO HORSES AND PEDESTRIANS.

Contents

ROUTE GRADES
▲ = MEDIUM ▲ = HARD ▲ = EXTREME (see page viii)

ROUTE TESTING IN TORRIDON PHOTO: PHIL MCKANE

Introduction

In the past few years the popularity of mountain biking in Scotland has exploded with hundreds of thousands of riders visiting the trail centres of the 7Stanes. My aim with this guidebook was to get away from the purpose built singletrack and into the wild places of Scotland.

The routes within the book cover the length and breadth of the country and hopefully provide something for all types of rider. There are short sweet loops close to Glasgow and Edinburgh which are perfect for escaping from the city for an hour or two. The easy rides are in stunning areas, giving routes which deliver spectacular scenery and wild landscapes without too many technical challenges along the way. The majority of the trips emphasise the kind of riding which I love – the big days out in remote and spectacular terrain, taking on technical singletrack, big climbs and the odd bit of traditional Scottish bog trotting!

Writing the book has been an immensely enjoyable experience for me. I have explored some areas of the country where I hadn't done much riding before and revisited some old classics which I'd not ridden in a long time. These are some of my favourite routes in the country, and I hope that any one of them will make you say "That was one of the best mountain bike rides I've ever done".

This book just scratches the surface of Scottish riding – there are enough trails to keep a mountain biker happy for a lifetime. Ride some of these routes, then get your maps out and start exploring!

Phil McKane

Acknowledgements

This book has come about with the input of many people. Thanks must go to John and the guys at Vertebrate Publishing along with everyone who suggested routes, rode them in the rain and made the coffee.

How to Use This Book
Mountain Biking in Scotland

Simply put, Scotland is home to some of the best mountain biking in the world. If you haven't ridden in Scotland, you really should. Named a 'Global Superstar' by the International Mountain Biking Association (IMBA) on a number of occasions, the variety of terrain, the locations and the jaw-dropping scenery mean Scotland is an incredible place to ride.

The Routes

The 25 routes in this guidebook cover the full gamut of Scottish mountain biking. There are short routes, within range of Glasgow and Edinburgh, mid-range routes in wonderful locations and multi-day adventures that you'll remember for the rest of your life.

Grades

Routes, climbs and descents are graded blue, red and black (and double-black!), in a similar system to that used at trail centres around the UK.

▲ = Easy ▲ = Moderate ▲ = Hard

The grades are based on average conditions – good weather and not too wet and muddy. Grades consider technicality, length, climbs, navigation and remoteness – so one 'black' route might be a short all-out technical test, while another could be a big endurance challenge with tricky navigation, some distance from civilisation. As ever, these grades are subjective. How you find a particular route, downhill or climb will be dictated by your own levels of fitness and skill.

Directions & Accuracy

While every effort has been made to ensure accuracy of information within the directions in this guide, things change and we are unable to guarantee that every detail will be correct. Please treat stated distances as guidelines. **Please exercise caution if a direction appears at odds with the route in the ground. A comparison between direction and map should see you on the right track**.

Access Law

Historically, Scotland's landowners have usually had a permissive attitude towards those wishing to access the countryside for the purposes of outdoor recreation, especially when compared to the situation in other parts of the UK. With the passing of the Land Reform (Scotland) Act in 2005, it is now set out in law that individuals have the right to access most land for recreational purposes, provided that this right is exercised responsibly. The key words are 'most land' and 'responsibly'. Places such as gardens, sports grounds and fields of crops are exempt. Acting responsibly means keeping speed under control in places where you are likely to come across walkers and other trail users, and avoiding areas where you are likely to cause damage, for example, very soft terrain. Hopefully, common sense should give sufficient direction, but the Scottish Outdoor Access Code aims to give extra guidance: **www.outdooraccess-scotland.com**

Estate Activities

Despite many people's stance against blood sports, shooting remains an important source of income for Highland estates and provides employment for rural communities. As mountain bikers, many of the tracks we ride are built and maintained by the estates to provide easier access to the hills for shooting parties. As part of exercising our right to access the countryside responsibly, we must take the interests of these landowners into account.

At the time of writing, **Red Deer stalking season** runs from 1 July to 20 October for stags, and from 21 October to 15 February for hinds. The majority of stalking involves stags, with August to October seeing the most activity. Similarly, grouse shooting begins on 12 August, running until 10 December, with most activity earlier in the season.

Within this period, individual estates will have their own stalking times, so please use Hillphones to find out where stalking is taking place before planning your route. Hillphones give a frequently updated recorded message with forecasts of stalking activity over the next few days. The service is run by Scottish Natural Heritage and the Mountaineering Council of Scotland. The areas covered and phone numbers can be found at **www.snh.org.uk/hillphones.** Alternatively, the office for each of the Highland Estates will also be able to give the relevant information, and is useful for local knowledge such as the state of tracks and depth of rivers. Their phone numbers are included with the individual routes.

Weather & Terrain

Billy Connolly once said that Scotland had just two seasons – June and winter. While the weather is not quite that bad, there is an element of truth in this. It's possible to experience very severe weather at any time of the year, and you must be prepared and equipped to deal with this. Many of the routes in this book are in high-level wilderness terrain, a long way from any kind of shelter from the elements. It pays to think more like a mountaineer than a cyclist in terms of clothing and equipment. For all remote rides full waterproofs should be carried. A mountaineering type jacket with taped seams and a proper hood gives much better protection than most cycling-specific waterproofs. Waterproof overtrousers may not be worn on the bike, but are essential for protecting the legs if you stop for any length of time. Similarly, an extra layer of warm clothing, a hat and spare gloves are indispensable at any time of year, as is a survival bag, and/or group shelter. A small headlight is also vital in case you run out of daylight due to accident or mechanical breakdown.

Along with suitable clothing and equipment you must have the skills to look after yourself and other members of your party when out in the wilds. Make sure you can fix common bike problems, can make sensible decisions on stream crossings and can navigate in poor visibility using a map and compass. If you have any doubts about your ability to operate safely in remote terrain, either hire a guide or book a wilderness skills course to learn the techniques under the instruction of an experienced tutor.

Midges

The midge is Scotland's most feared predator and strikes terror into the heart of many mountain bikers! It is likely that you will encounter the blood thirsty creatures between May and September, although July and August are the worst months. The female is responsible for biting as the blood is necessary for the development of her eggs. Fortunately midges can only fly at about 1mph, so they're not much of a problem when you're actually riding your bike. However, if you stop to have lunch or fix a mechanical, they can be unbearable. Insect repellents containing DEET are reasonably effective, though the active ingredient is pretty nasty stuff and will damage plastic if it comes into contact with your sunglasses or watchstrap for example. Highlanders of old used sprigs of bog myrtle in their clothing to keep the midges at bay and some of the chemical-free repellents contain extracts of this herb. The most effective method is to keep any exposed skin covered, and a midge head net, while looking a bit daft, can be worth its weight in gold.

Bothies

Bothies are unlocked shelters in remote locations throughout Scotland where hill walkers, climbers and mountain bikers are able to spend the night. They range from rough stone shelters to disued cottages with several rooms. The Mountain Bothies Association is a registered charity taking care of around 100 bothies. Visit **www.mountainbothies.org.uk** for more information.

General Safety

The ability to read a map, navigate in poor visibility and to understand weather warnings is essential. Don't head out in bad weather, unless you're confident and capable of doing so.

Some of the routes described point you at tough climbs and steep descents that can potentially be very dangerous. Too much exuberance on a steep descent in the middle of nowhere and you could be in more than a spot of bother, especially if you're alone. Consider your limitations and relative fragility.

Be self-sufficient. Carry food and water, spares, a tube and a pump. Consider a first-aid kit. Pack full lights if you think you could finish in the dark.

If you're riding solo, think about the seriousness of an accident – you might be without help for a very long time. Tell someone where you're going, when you'll be back and tell them once you are back. Take a mobile phone if you have one, but don't expect a signal. And don't call out the ambulance because you've grazed your knee.

Riding in a group is safer and often more fun, but don't leave slower riders too far behind and give them a minute for a breather when they've caught up. Allow extra time for a group ride, as you'll inevitably stop and chat. Ride within you're ability, make sure you can slow down fast and give way to other users. Bells might be annoying but they work. If you can't bring yourself to bolt one on, then a polite 'excuse me' should be fine. On hot, sunny days, slap on some factor 30+ and **ALWAYS WEAR YOUR HELMET!**

In the Event of an Accident

In the event of an accident requiring immediate assistance: Dial **999** and ask for **POLICE – MOUNTAIN RESCUE**. If you can provide details of your location, including grid reference, this will speed up their response time.

Rules of the (Off) Road

1. Always ride on legal trails.
2. Ride considerately – give way to horses and pedestrians.
3. Don't spook animals.
4. Ride in control – you don't know who's around the next corner.
5. Leave gates as you find them – if you're unsure, shut them.
6. Keep the noise down and don't swear loudly when you fall off in front of walkers.
7. Leave no trace – take home everything you took out.
8. Keep water sources clean – don't take toilet stops near streams.
9. Enjoy the countryside and respect its life and work.

Planning Your Ride

1. Consider the ability/experience of each rider in your group. Check the weather forecast. How much time do you have available? Now choose your route.
2. Study the route description before setting off, and cross-reference it with the relevant map.
3. Bear in mind everything we've suggested about safety, clothing, spares and food and drink.
4. Get out there and get dirty.

Maps & Symbols

Ordnance Survey maps are the most commonly used, are easy to read and many people are happy using them. If you're not familiar with OS maps and are unsure of what the symbols mean, you can download a free map legend from **www.v-outdoor.co.uk**

Here's a guide to the symbols and abbreviations we use on the maps and in our directions:

⑤→ ROUTE STARTING POINT	**▲** MEDIUM ASCENT	**⋀** MEDIUM DESCENT	**ABBREVIATIONS USED IN ROUTE DIRECTIONS**
⑤→ ALTERNATIVE STARTING POINT	**▲** HARD ASCENT	**⋀** HARD DESCENT	**L** = Left
◆→ OPTIONAL ROUTE	**▲** VERY HARD ASCENT	**⋀** VERY HARD DESCENT	**R** = Right
2 STAGE MARKER	**←◯◯** LINK TO ANOTHER ROUTE	**SA** = Straight Ahead	**G.O.A.P.** = Get Off And Push

Gaelic Translations

Maps of Scotland are full of Gaelic words, or their anglicised versions, that are used to describe places or features of the terrain. This list contains a few of the most commonly used words and their translations to help you understand what the map is telling you.

Abhainn	river	Dearg	red
Alba	Scotland	Dubh	black, dark
Allt	stream	Gaick	cleft
Baine	white	Garbh	rough
Beag	small	Hourn	Hell
Bealach	mountain pass	Loch	lake
Beinn, Ben	mountain	Lochan	small lake or pond
Beithe	birch tree	Mor, Mhor	large, big
Monadh	mountain range	Nevis	Heaven
Bothain	bothy	Sgor	sharp jagged rock
Cairn	pile of stones	Stane	stone
Clach	stone		

SECTION 1

Southern & Central Scotland

Southern and Central Scotland is home to most of the country's population, but it is by no means crowded. Great mountain bike routes can be found starting in the suburbs of Edinburgh and Glasgow, and fantastic wilderness trails can be found just a short journey from these cities.

Southern & Central Scotland
sponsored by

www.sealskinz.com

MUGDOCK PARK, GLASGOW

DESCENDING LOWTHER HILL, NEAR WANLOCKHEAD

Southern & Central Scotland
route finder

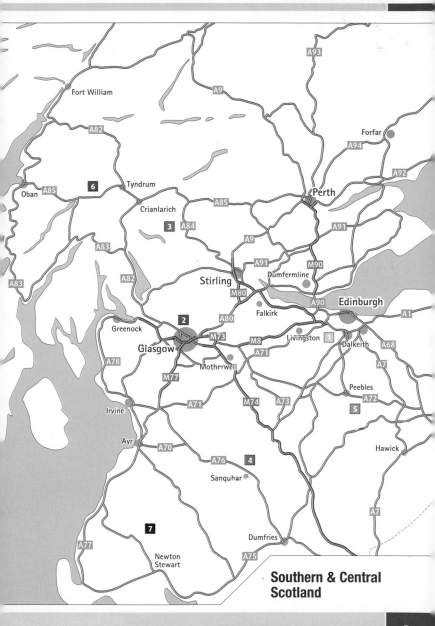

Southern & Central Scotland

01 **The Pentland Hills** – Edinburgh   16.5km

Introduction

The Pentland Hills have a real remote, big mountain feel, despite being within easy riding distance of the city of Edinburgh. They are the perfect destination for everything from a quick blast to blow away the cobwebs, to an all day epic. Due to their proximity to the city, the trails bear a heavy burden of mountain bikers and other outdoor enthusiasts, and some trails are susceptible to damage in very wet conditions. This route covers tracks that drain well in the wet, and remain rideable on a year–round basis.

The Ride

Starting at Harlaw Visitor Centre, a short tarmac section allows for a warm-up before the first climb up Cock Rig. A gravelly track leads to the top of Maidens Cleugh and a high-speed rocky descent down to Glencorse Reservoir. A tarmac lane along the side of Logan Burn leads to Loganlea Reservoir before the singletrack starts again. In Green Cleugh it's easy to forget you're only a few miles from Edinburgh as the rugged hills tower steeply up and the trail winds by waterfalls and splashes through the burn. At Bavelaw Castle a fantastic rooty singletrack descent runs parallel to the road before a spin along the edge of Threipmuir Reservoir leads back to the start.

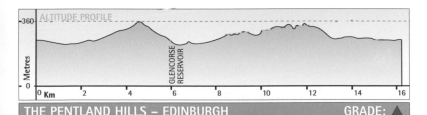

THE PENTLAND HILLS – EDINBURGH   **GRADE:** ▲

TOTAL DISTANCE: 16.5KM » **TOTAL ASCENT**: 420M » **TIME**: 1.5–2.5 HOURS » **START/FINISH**: CAR PARK, HARLAW RESERVOIR » **START GRID REF**: NT 182655 » **SATNAV**: EH14 7AS » **OS MAP**: LANDRANGER 66 **CONTACT**: PENTLAND HILLS REGIONAL PARK TEL: 0131 445 3383 » **CAFÉ**: NONE ON ROUTE

⟳ Take the road towards Harlaw Farm and turn **R** towards Wester Kinleith.

2 After the farm at Wester Kinleith, turn **R** onto the rocky track heading uphill. There is some rooty singletrack through the trees to the left of the main track, but the ground is very soft. It's best avoided unless very dry or frozen.

3 At the junction go through the gate and follow the gravel track as it climbs uphill. There are several wooden water bars on this section. Please don't make the path any wider by riding around the sides of these – use a well-timed bunnyhop instead!

4 At the top of Maidens Cleugh go through the gate, and then drop your saddle for the fantastic descent to Glencorse. It is rutted at the top, has some big tricky drainage channels in the fast middle section and becomes rocky just before the finish.

5 Turn **R** onto the single lane tarmac road at Glencorse Reservoir. Follow this along the Logan Burn to The Howe at the western end of Loganlea Reservoir.

6 The track branches in several directions at The Howe. Take the riverside track to Green Cleugh, signposted *Balerno*. This is grassy, and boggy in places at first, but becomes good gravel singletrack in the narrow valley between Black Hill and Hare Hill.

7 At Bavelaw Castle go through the gate and join the tarmac road. The road makes a 90° **L** turn followed soon after by a 90° **R** turn. On the outside of the right turn a fantastic narrow singletrack winds down the left side of the road, between the trees and the drainage ditch. Rejoin the tarmac and cross the reservoir at Redford Bridge.

8 Pick up the singletrack through Redford Wood, and follow the track beside Threipmuir and Harlaw Reservoirs back to the start. There is some rooty singletrack right on the waters edge, but again this is susceptible to damage in all but the driest conditions.

←⊙⊙ **Making a day of it**

The Pentland Hills are criss-crossed with miles of trails that can be combined to make for epic days out. This route could be extended to include Allermuir Hill and Phantom's Cleugh to the north east or the Kipps, North Esk Reservoir and the Bore Stane to the south west. Be prepared to alter your route depending on the conditions on the ground and if in doubt, phone the Ranger Service for advice.

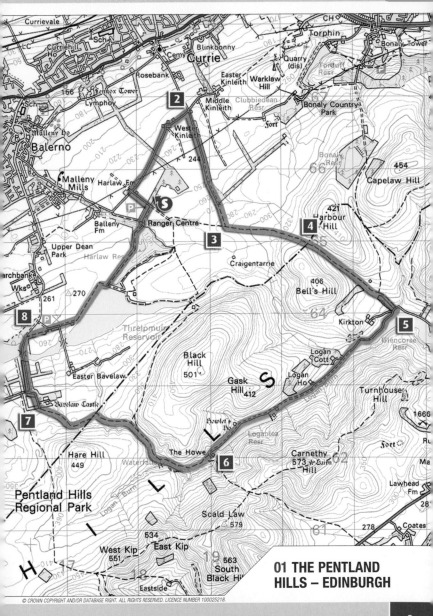

01 THE PENTLAND HILLS – EDINBURGH

© CROWN COPYRIGHT AND/OR DATABASE RIGHT. ALL RIGHTS RESERVED. LICENCE NUMBER 100025218.

02 **Mugdock Park** – Glasgow   6.5km

Introduction

Mugdock Country Park on the outskirts of Glasgow is a real haven for the city's mountain bikers. It has an amazing number of singletrack trails in a small area and is a great starting point for longer days out. Being close to the city, it is popular with families and dog walkers and can get busy on weekends. However, it is easy to avoid the crowds as Mugdock is a great destination for night riding and is a regular haunt for Glasgow mountain bikers after dark. This very short, sweet loop takes in some of the park's best singletrack trails and is perfect for a quick blast in the evening.

The Ride

Mugdock Visitor Centre with its gift shop and tearoom acts as the starting point for this ride. Easy trails lead to the ruins of Mugdock Castle which dates back to around the 14th century. From the castle a fantastic descent leads to a section of the West Highland Way, from which a challenging stretch of singletrack twists and turns above the Allander Water and is the real highlight of the loop. A steep and loose, but fortunately short, climb marks the beginning of the return leg which then climbs back up the previous descent. All but the most gifted bike handlers will be off and pushing the last section back to the castle, before returning to the tearoom for a well-earned cuppa!

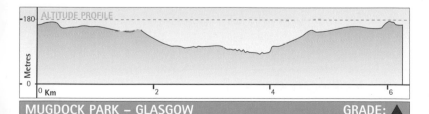

ALTITUDE PROFILE

Metres — 180 — 0

0 Km   2   4   6

MUGDOCK PARK – GLASGOW   **GRADE:** ▲

TOTAL DISTANCE: 6.5KM » **TOTAL ASCENT**: 100M » **TIME**: 1 HOUR » **START/FINISH**: MUGDOCK VISITOR CENTRE
START GRID REF: NS 547780 » **SATNAV**: G62 8EL » **OS MAP**: LANDRANGER 64 » **CONTACT**: MUGDOCK PARK RANGER
SERVICE TEL: 0141 956 6586 » **CAFÉ**: STABLES TEAROOM TEL: 0141 956 6100

1 From the Visitor Centre, follow the signposts towards Mugdock Castle.

2 At the castle, turn **R** and then shortly after **R** again, onto a section of boardwalk trail. This is signposted *Drumclog Moor / West Highland Way*.

3 Squeeze through the narrow gap in the stone wall and start descending. This downhill is rocky and technical towards the top before flattening out into a fast boardwalk section. There are several sets of raised planks on this section, so keep your speed in check. The pairs are about one bike length apart making them very difficult to bunnyhop!

4 At the fork in the trail take the **R** branch and continue on to meet up with the West Highland Way. Turn **R** onto this, keeping an eye out to the left for the next section of singletrack, which runs parallel to the main track.

5 Turn sharp **L** onto the singletrack approx 50m before the West Highland Way crosses the road. Follow this excellent technical singletrack above the river. The singletrack rejoins the main track at a signpost. Climb the steep hill to the junction. Turn **R** and retrace the outward route back towards Mugdock Castle and the Visitor Centre.

← **Making a day of it**

Mugdock Country Park has an amazing number of trails, most of which are not marked on any maps. It is easy to spend a whole day there exploring the tracks you find and combining them together into several short loops. A longer expedition up the West Highland Way to Glengoyne Distillery and back via the Campsie Fells makes a good half-day ride, with the option of a wee dram in the middle!

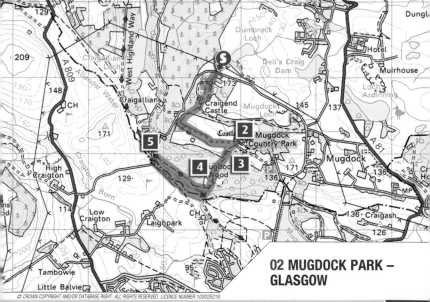

02 MUGDOCK PARK – GLASGOW

© CROWN COPYRIGHT AND/OR DATABASE RIGHT. ALL RIGHTS RESERVED. LICENCE NUMBER 100025218.

03 **Glen Finglas** – The Trossachs

28km

Introduction

Around an hour north of Glasgow, Glen Finglas in the picturesque Trossachs was once a medieval hunting ground, favoured by the Stewart Kings of Scotland. Today the glen is owned by the Woodland Trust who are attempting to restore the native woodland and conserve the glen's natural wild state. This route takes in Glen Finglas and the neighbouring Glen Meann as it loops around 'The Mell', the 674m Meall Cala. The route follows a well surfaced Landrover track for its full duration and presents no real technical challenges. However, it does go a long way from civilisation and – almost reaching 600m – can be subject to severe weather. On a clear day, the views of the surrounding hills and lochs are nothing short of spectacular.

The Ride

From the Woodland Trust car park, just east of Brig o' Turk, the route climbs above the valley on a stony trail that gives fantastic views of Loch Venachar and beyond. A farm road rises and falls along the banks of the reservoir, becoming a rough stony track soon after Ben Ledi cottage. The trail splits where the glens Meann and Finglas meet, and a long and sustained climb round the back of Meall Cala leads to the high point of the route at almost 600m. The reward for all the hard work is a long, fast and steep descent to the head of Glen Finglas. Returning down the glen means more descending, with a few short counter climbs, to the excellent tearoom amongst the pretty cottages of Brig o' Turk.

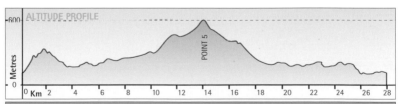

GLEN FINGLAS – THE TROSSACHS

GRADE: ▲»▲

TOTAL DISTANCE: 28KM » **TOTAL ASCENT:** 1000M » **TIME:** 3–4 HOURS » **START/FINISH:** WOODLAND TRUST CAR PARK
START GRID REF: NN 546065 » **SATNAV:** BRIG O' TURK » **OS MAP:** LANDRANGER 57 » **CAFE:** BRIG O' TURK TEA ROOM
TEL: 01877 376267

Directions – Glen Finglas – The Trossachs

⤷ From the Woodland Trust car park, cross the bridge and turn **L** after the gate, following the orange-ringed marker posts. The trail climbs steeply and is a real test of the ability to keep enough weight on each wheel to maintain both traction and steering control.

2 On meeting the tarmac reservoir access road, turn **R** and follow it past the dam and along the banks of the reservoir. The tarmac gives way to a well-surfaced Landrover track, shortly after Ben Ledi Cottage, which continues to the junction with Glen Meann.

3 At the fork turn **R** signed *Hill Path to Balquidder*. This track climbs into Glen Meann following the river and crossing several contributory streams that run off the western side of Ben Vane.

4 At the junction turn **R** uphill, keeping the fence on your left-hand side. (**Note:** This junction is poorly represented on the OS map, with the footpath to Balquidder actually branching off from further up the hill.)

5 The high point of the route! There is a cairn at the side of the track that signifies the highest point of the climb. This is a good time to drop your saddle in anticipation of the forthcoming downhill. The descent is fast and open with big sweeping corners and hidden surprises. Be aware that cattle do graze on the hillside and can be on the track!

6 Bridge over the Finglas Water. It is possible to blast straight through the ford, but it can get quite deep after heavy rain. There is a bridge upstream for those wanting to avoid wet feet.

7 Rejoin the original track alongside the reservoir. This time follow the tarmac into the village. (The tearoom is situated at the junction with the main road.) Turn **L** and follow the A821 for 1km back to the car park.

**03 GLEN FINGLAS –
THE TROSSACHS**

© CROWN COPYRIGHT AND/OR DATABASE RIGHT. ALL RIGHTS RESERVED. LICENCE NUMBER 100025218.

04 **Southern Upland Way &**
The Dempster Road   30km

Introduction

The Southern Upland Way is a long distance route that traverses southern Scotland from coast to coast. This route heads east on a section of the SUW between the Mennock Pass, near San-quhar, and Wanlockhead, returning via moorland tracks and a fantastic single-track trail known as the Dempster Road. Wanlockhead is the highest village in Scotland. It has a history of lead mining which is still evident today, and which has provided a network of old mine roads that make for excellent mountain biking. As well as lead, there are deposits of gold in the hills so you might well meet a few enthusiasts panning for their fortunes in the many small burns!

The Ride

The route starts from the Mennock Pass and climbs over Auchentaggart Moor to meet up with the Southern Upland Way. The first half of the route has steep grassy climbs and high speed open descents. On crossing the Wanlock Water you pass the old mine workings and restored Beam Engine on the way into the village. The Lead Mining Museum's superb tearoom is perfect for refuelling, before the stiff climb up Lowther Hill. From here exposed moorland tracks skirt East Mount Lowther and Threehope Height before the highlight of the ride. The Dempster Road is a superb narrow singletrack trail that cuts through the heather on the steep hillside as it drops back to the Mennock Pass.

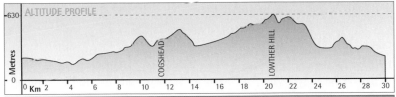

SOUTHERN UPLAND WAY & THE DEMPSTER ROAD   GRADE: ▲

TOTAL DISTANCE: 30KM » **TOTAL ASCENT**: 1200M » **TIME**: 3-5 HOURS » **START/FINISH**: PARKING AREA, THE MENNOCK PASS » **START GRID REF**: NS 850104 » **SATNAV**: SANQUHAR » **OS MAP**: LANDRANGER 71
CAFÉ: LEAD MINING MUSEUM, WANLOCKHEAD TEL: 01659 74387

© CROWN COPYRIGHT AND/OR DATABASE RIGHT. ALL RIGHTS RESERVED. LICENCE NUMBER 100025218.

04 SOUTHERN UPLAND WAY & THE DEMPSTER ROAD

Directions – Southern Upland Way & The Dempster Road

⑤► Start at the roadside parking area in the Mennock Pass, the B797 between Sanquhar and Wanlockhead (NS 850104). From here, head downhill (west) along the tarmac road towards Sanquhar.

④S► Starting in Sanquhar, which has a railway station, and following the Southern Upland Way from the town to where it joins the loop adds 6km and 150m of climbing to the route.

2 Turn **R** onto a singletrack tarmac road. There is a brown Tourist Information road sign (*Lead Mining Museum 6 miles*) at the junction. Follow this road uphill.

3 After 750m the road branches, turn **L** here, through a gate and onto a roughly surfaced, slightly downhill track. The surface deteriorates and becomes rocky as you climb. Take care passing through Brandleys farm as there may be farm vehicles operating.

4 As the dry stone wall on the left turns away from the track turn **R** to join the Southern Upland Way. This is marked with a small marker post. Cross the stile and climb past the small patch of trees. Follow the marker posts as the track climbs for around 2km. This is steep but mostly rideable apart from one short section (400m) towards the top. From the high point of the climb a fast open descent with some tight bends brings you to Cogshead.

5 Turn **R** onto the forest road and right again after 250m following the SUW signs. There are some short sections of singletrack on this part of the trail as well as wooden bridges spanning the burns. (North Shore, Southern Uplands style!) From Glengaber Hill, a fast twisty descent drops down to Wanlock Water, where you can splash through the ford or keep your feet dry on the bridge.

6 After crossing the river, turn **R** and follow the track past the old mine workings and the restored Beam Engine. The track becomes tarmac approaching Wanlockhead where the Lead Mining Museum tearoom beckons.

7 From the Museum, climb steeply uphill, passing the Youth Hostel to the B797. Cross the road and climb towards the radio masts and giant golf ball on Lowther Hill.

8 After 3km of climbing, turn **R** onto the stony track opposite the radio mast. Follow this track as it skirts the west flank of East Mount Lowther. **The track is indistinct in places and it is important to pay attention to navigation in this section as it is easy to lose the trail and become disorientated on this featureless hillside.**

9 After just over 2km the track forks (NS 870094). Take the **L** fork and follow the ridge above Lang Cleuch for 850m. **(Note: This junction is not marked on the OS map.)**

10 The track branches again at NS 868085, this time take the **R** fork. **(Again, this is not marked on the OS map.)** Descend, aiming for the corner of the dry stone wall and cross Auchenlone Burn at the rocky ford.

11 Turn **R** and follow the grassy track along the edge of the fallen wall towards the ruined farm at Glenim.

12 Cross the burn on the stony track after the farm and then turn **R** uphill. Go through the gate and climb up the side of Cock Hill.

13 The track branches at a sheepfold. Take the **R** fork towards the pass and the top of the Dempster Road.

14 The Dempster Road has several options for the descent. All are fantastic skinny ribbons of singletrack through the heather. Balance, finesse and concentration are required if you are not to be pitched down the steep hillside! Whichever option you take, aim for the sheepfold at NS 865099.

15 From the sheepfold go approx 50m upstream and cross the river onto a gravelly track. Follow this to the road, turn **L** and return to the start.

Introduction

The Tweed Valley is famous in the world of mountain biking as the home of two of Scotland's premier 7Stanes trail centres, Glentress and Innerleithen. Look beyond the manufactured singletrack and you'll find the area is criss-crossed by miles and miles of trails that are all superb for mountain biking. This ride mixes the 7Stanes Traquair XC trail at Innerleithen with old drovers routes and natural singletrack that traverse the surrounding hills. As such, it is a fantastic combination of both the old and the new in Scottish mountain biking.

The Ride

Starting at the 7Stanes car park in Innerleithen, the route initially follows the Traquair XC trail until it meets the Southern Upland Way on the Minch Moor. The route then heads east out of the forest on the old drove road towards the Three Brethren, three enormous cairns on the edge of Yair Hill Forest. A sharp descent towards Broadmeadows Youth Hostel and Yarrowford allows some respite before the long climb of the Minch Moor Road. Take time to savour the view of the rolling Borders hills before heading back into the forest for the rest of the Traquair trail, finishing with the fabulous Caddon Bank descent.

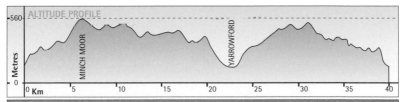

THE MINCH MOOR – INNERLEITHEN   **GRADE:** ▲

TOTAL DISTANCE: 40KM » **TOTAL ASCENT**: 1100M » **TIME**: 4–6 HOURS » **START/FINISH**: 7STANES CAR PARK, INNERLEITHEN » **START GRID REF**: NT 334360 » **SATNAV**: EH44 6PD » **OS MAP**: LANDRANGER 73
PUB: TRAQUAIR ARMS HOTEL TEL: 01896 830 229 » **BIKE SHOP**: ALPINE BIKES, INNERLEITHEN TEL: 01896 830 880

© CROWN COPYRIGHT AND/OR DATABASE RIGHT. ALL RIGHTS RESERVED. LICENCE NUMBER 100025218.

05 THE MINCH MOOR – INNERLEITHEN

Directions – The Minch Moor – Innerleithen

➏➤ Start at the Innerleithen 7Stanes car park. Follow the Traquair XC trail to the top of the Minch Moor climb and descend to the junction with the forest road at marker post 24.

2 At the marker post turn **R** onto the Southern Upland Way and descend on a grassy track, crossing the next forest road and continuing up a grassy climb to the fork in the trail at a Southern Upland Way signpost. This section can be slippery and a little boggy in the wet, but is still generally rideable.

3 At the signpost, fork **L** and climb over the summit of Brown Knowe. The descent from the summit is a cracker – an extremely fast and rocky straight line plummet that gets steeper towards the bottom as it approaches a small patch of woods.

4 Cross the stile and follow the grassy track that climbs over Broomy Law towards Yair Hill Forest and the Three Brethren. The views from this section, over the surrounding hills stretching out into the distance are quite spectacular.

5 At the Three Brethren, follow the Southern Upland Way downhill for approximately 1km as it runs along the side of a fence to a gate above Long Philip Burn.

6 Go through the gate, turn **R** – leaving the Southern Upland Way – and follow a feint path that runs back along the opposite side of the fence in the other direction. Shortly after the fence turns back uphill a narrow track leads off to the **L**. The start of this track is difficult to find, but it becomes better defined as it crosses the hillside and drops down to a gate. From the gate, the path over the north flank of Foulshiels Hill becomes obvious.

7 From the top of the climb another fast and rocky descent drops down to the woods around Broadmeadows Youth Hostel, and then the main road.

8 Turn **R** and follow the road for 1km, through the village of Yarrowford. Turn **R** after the phone box in the village, signposted *The Minch Moor*. Engage your climbing legs as the tarmac turns to gravel track beyond the houses. The trail swings round to the left and climbs steeply, up the grassy ridge above the burn. The soft grassy surface is heavy going, but following the green *Tweed Trails* signs makes navigation simple.

9 After a long grind to the top of the Minch Moor turn **L** and follow the Southern Upland Way back into the forest. Rejoin the Traquair XC trail and mix with the armour-clad downhillers on the fantastic Caddon Bank descent back to the car park.

06 **Glen Kinglass** – Bridge of Orchy   57km

Introduction

Glen Kinglass runs from Loch Tulla at the southern end of Rannoch Moor towards Loch Etive, a sea loch that stretches some 30km inland from the Firth of Lorn. This is a point-to-point route that can be linked using the West Highland Railway line. From Tyndrum the route takes the old military road that now forms part of the West Highland Way. At Bridge of Orchy, Glen Kinglass heads deep into the rugged mountains of Lorn which lie between the main Glasgow to Fort William road and Loch Etive. This is a well maintained estate and gives a long but inspiring wilderness ride. From the mouth of the River Kinglass, seals may well be spotted in the water on the lochside finale to Taynuilt.

The Ride

From Lower Tyndrum railway station, the section to Bridge of Orchy is covered on the well-surfaced tracks of the West Highland Way. After an initial climb out of the village, this route follows the railway line to Bridge of Orchy. Crossing the main road and following the single lane tarmac leads to Victoria Bridge, where you leave civilisation behind and follow the Abhainn Shira to Loch Dochard and Glen Kinglass. There's a real variety of terrain through the glen, from smooth estate roads to rocky singletrack and Moab-style exposed bedrock (almost!). On reaching Loch Etive at Ardmaddy, a good Landrover track takes you south, crossing the River Liver and River Noe on the way to the railway station at Taynuilt.

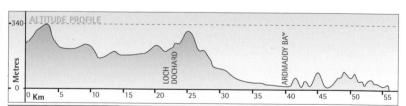

GLEN KINGLASS – BRIDGE OF ORCHY   **GRADE:** ▲

DISTANCE: 57KM » **TOTAL ASCENT**: 1100M » **TIME**: 5-7 HOURS » **START**: TYNDRUM LOWER RAILWAY STATION
START GRID REF: NN 327301 » **START SATNAV**: FK20 8RZ » **FINISH**: TAYNUILT RAILWAY STATION
FINISH GRID REF: NN 003313 » **FINISH SATNAV**: PA35 1JH » **OS MAP**: LANDRANGER 50 » **CONTACT**: GLENKINGLASS
STALKER TEL: 01866 822271. SCOTRAIL TEL: 08457 55 00 33 » **PUB**: BRIDGE OF ORCHY HOTEL TEL: 01838 400208

Directions – Glen Kinglass – Bridge of Orchy

➎ From the station pick up the *West Highland Way* signposts, following them through the village before climbing to the bridge across the railway line beside the main road. Carry on along the West Highland Way to Bridge of Orchy.

➏ By starting at Bridge of Orchy it is possible to reduce the distance cycled by 12km and the height climbed by 200m. This does however require careful co-ordination of the train timetables, and a change of train between Lower Tyndrum and Upper Tyndrum stations.

2 Cross the main road (A82) at the Bridge of Orchy Hotel, and follow the single lane tarmac road to Victoria Bridge. (The West Highland Way cuts the corner climbing over Mam Carraigh, but this is boggy and best avoided on a bike.)

3 Cross Victoria Bridge and take the track just before Forest Lodge, signposted *Public Footpath to Loch Etive by Glen Kinglass*.

4 The track becomes less well travelled towards Loch Dochard, but the mountain scenery really opens up, with fantastic views towards Stob Coir an Albannaich and Glas Bheinn Mhor.

5 The area around the footbridge across the head of the River Kinglass is quite boggy. **The estate has requested that the old footbridge marked on the map isn't used. A new bridge has been constructed approximately 400m downstream**. The trail passes several waterfalls on the river as it makes its way to Glenkinglass Lodge, which can be seen sitting in a group of trees across the river.

6 From the Lodge, a well surfaced Landrover track follows the river for 10.5km to Loch Etive at Ardmaddy Bay.

7 A well surfaced track undulates above Loch Etive for 10km. Short sharp climbs and descents signal the crossings of Glen Liver and Glen Noe, before entering the forest and reaching Inverawe House.

8 Follow the minor tarmac road to the main road. Turn **R** and follow the A85 for 4km to the railway station at Taynuilt.

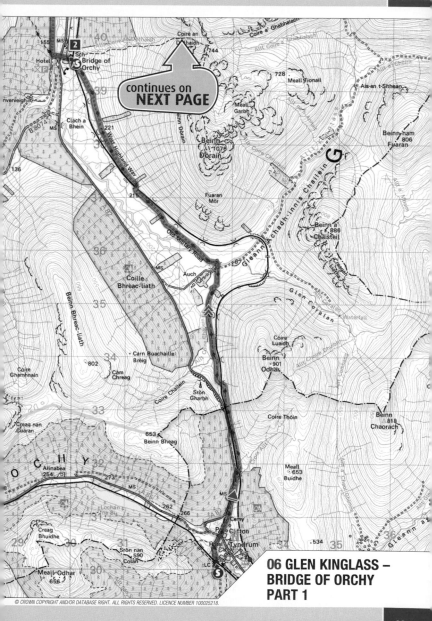

continues on
NEXT PAGE

06 GLEN KINGLASS –
BRIDGE OF ORCHY
PART 1

© CROWN COPYRIGHT AND/OR DATABASE RIGHT. ALL RIGHTS RESERVED. LICENCE NUMBER 100025218.

continues on
NEXT PAGE

© CROWN COPYRIGHT AND/OR DATABASE RIGHT. ALL RIGHTS RESERVED. LICENCE NUMBER 100025218.

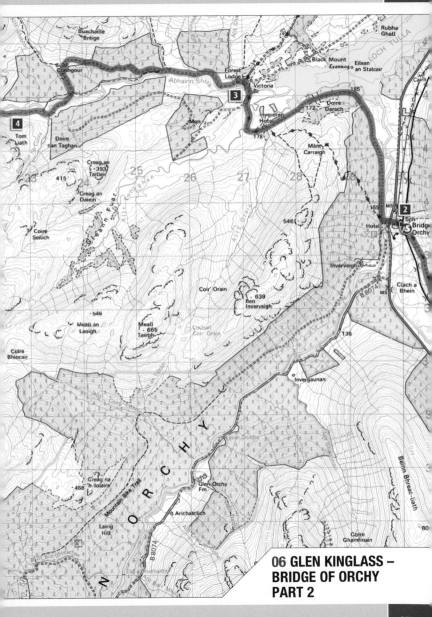

06 GLEN KINGLASS –
BRIDGE OF ORCHY
PART 2

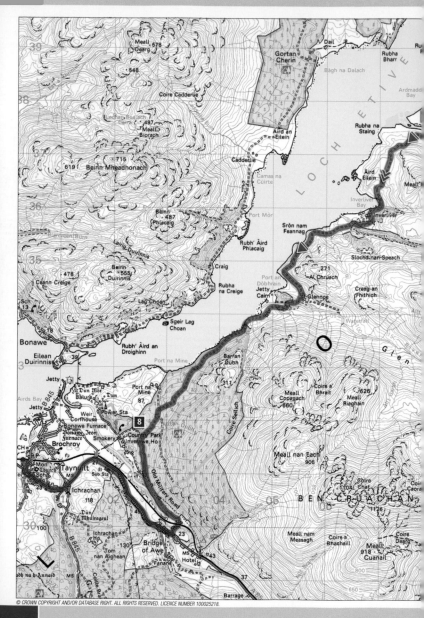

© CROWN COPYRIGHT AND/OR DATABASE RIGHT. ALL RIGHTS RESERVED. LICENCE NUMBER 100025218.

06 GLEN KINGLASS –
BRIDGE OF ORCHY
PART 3

Introduction

Glentrool Forest in Dumfries & Galloway has a long history as a mountain biking destination. One of the first Polaris Challenge mountain bike orienteering events was held in the forest in the early 1990s and today it is home to the Glentrool Big Country Route, part of the 7Stanes trail network. This two day expedition takes in much of the Big Country Route, along with some of the stunning scenery and great riding in the surrounding area. Using mainly forest tracks and minor roads it is a great expedition for those of modest technical ability, but there are diversions enroute to entertain even the most experienced of riders, and no one will be disappointed by the landscape.

The Ride

Starting the route at Stinchar Bridge puts the village of Minnigaff at roughly the halfway point and allows for an overnight stop at its youth hostel. The bothy at Blackhill of Bush provides a more remote overnight option, although the starting point would need to be adjusted to split the distance more evenly. The route follows minor roads over the rolling moor before meeting up with Sustrans Cycle Route No. 7. Following the cycle route through Glentrool Forest leads to the village and the start of the 7Stanes Big Country Loop. 7Stanes marker posts make for simple navigation all the way to Loch Dee, where more forestry tracks past Loch Doon and Loch Bradan lead back to the starting point.

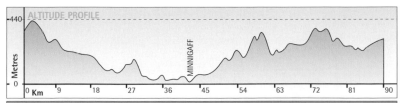

GLENTROOL TOUR

GRADE: ▲

DISTANCE: 90KM » **TOTAL ASCENT**: 2000M (APPROX) » **TIME**: 2 DAYS (4–6 HOURS PER DAY) » **START/FINISH**: FORESTRY CAR PARK, STINCHAR BRIDGE » **START GRID REF**: NX 397956 » **START SATNAV**: TALLAMINOCH (CLOSEST)
OS MAP: LANDRANGER 77 AND 83 » **CAFÉ**: KIRROUGHTREE HOUSE HOTEL TEL: 01671 402 141 YOUTH HOSTEL MINNIGAFF TEL: 01671 402 211

continues on
NEXT PAGE

© CROWN COPYRIGHT AND/OR DATABASE RIGHT. ALL RIGHTS RESERVED. LICENCE NUMBER 100025218.

07 GLENTROOL TOUR
PART 1

continues on
NEXT PAGE

© CROWN COPYRIGHT AND/OR DATABASE RIGHT. ALL RIGHTS RESERVED. LICENCE NUMBER 100025218.

continues on **PREVIOUS PAGE**

**07 GLENTROOL TOUR
PART 2**

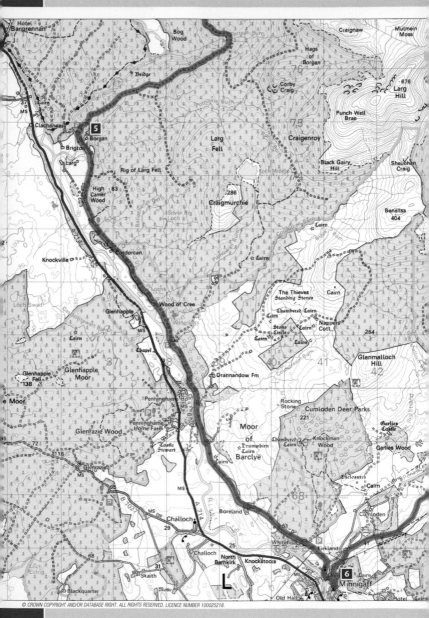

© CROWN COPYRIGHT AND/OR DATABASE RIGHT. ALL RIGHTS RESERVED. LICENCE NUMBER 100025218.

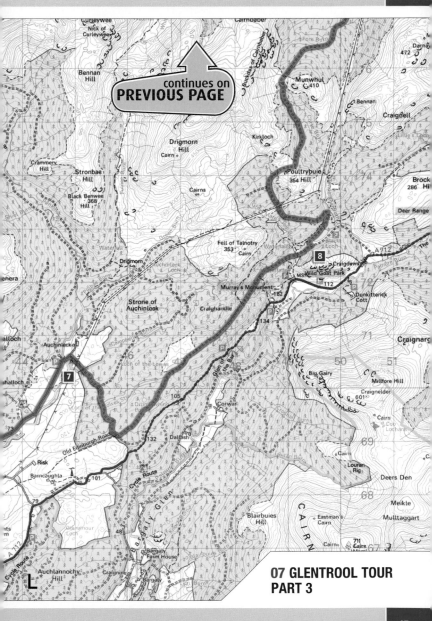

continues on PREVIOUS PAGE

07 GLENTROOL TOUR PART 3

Directions – Glentrool Tour

1 From the parking in Carrick Forest, cross Stinchar Bridge and head south for 7.5km.

2 At the Rowantree Toll junction, which was once the site of a tollhouse and inn, turn **L** onto Sustrans Route No. 7 and follow this for 13km through Glentrool Forest towards Glentrool Village.

3 Just before the village turn **L** onto a minor road that leads to Glentrool Visitor Centre and the 7Stanes trailhead.

4 Follow the 7Stanes Big Country Route marker posts past Caldons Campsite and Jenny's Hill, all the way to Borgan.

5 At Borgan turn **L** onto the minor road that follows the River Cree along the edge of the woods for 11km to Minnigaff. There are some nice views to the river and of the mixed woodland you are riding through along this section. Minnigaff has a beautiful old church and was a busy market village in its day.

6 From Minnigaff the route carries on for 6km on a single lane tarmac road, through Cumloden Deer Park towards Auchinleck.

7 Just after the Auchinleck Bridge turn **R**, passing under the power lines and into the forest. After 1.9km (Marker 30) turn **L**, picking up the Old Edinburgh Road and passing the Loch of the Lowes. Around 2km after the Loch (at Marker 32) the route meets the Black Craigs 7Stanes trail from Kirroughtree. Riding this black-graded singletrack loop would add 14km to the total distance. Otherwise carry on along the forest track to Black Loch.

8 At Black Loch continue following the 7Stanes marker posts past Poultrybuie Hill and Munwhul, meeting up with the minor road at Craigencallie.

9 Approximately 2km after Craigencallie House turn **R** and take the forest road, then turn **L** after the bridge over the Black Water of Dee.

10 Pass the two giant blocks known as Mc Whanns Stone and turn **L**, following the forest track past Blackhill of Bush bothy and on towards Riders Rig.

11 From Riders Rig, it is necessary to go 'off piste' for a short section through the forest fire breaks. As the track bends a muddy track leads off **L** through the firebreak. The track doubles back on itself initially before meeting with the forest road which runs along the east bank of Gala Lane and leads to the head of Loch Doon.

12 Cross the bridge over Gala Lane and follow the track around the south end of the loch for 2km.

13 Turn **L** at the track junction. Pass the *Carrick Forest Drive* sign and head towards Loch Bradan.

14 Turn **L** at the southern tip of Loch Bradan and follow the tarmac back to Stinchar Bridge.

SECTION 2

North West Scotland & Highlands

The landscape of the western half of Scotland is dramatic, a line of teeth facing out the on-coming Atlantic weather systems. Home to many of Scotland's highest peaks, this part of the country lends itself to demanding, but highly rewarding, mountain bike rides.

North West Scotland & Highlands sponsored by

LUMICYCLE
High Performance Cycle Lights
www.lumicycle.com

GLEN SLIGACHAN, ISLE OF SKYE

GLEN SLIGACHAN, ISLE OF SKYE

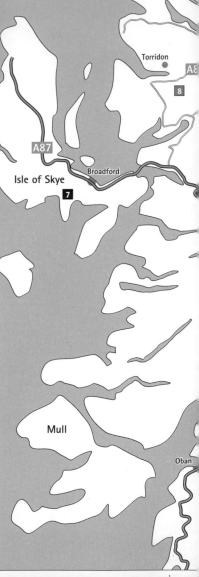

North West Scotland & Highlands
route finder

Loch Ness

Inverness

Aviemore

2

Fort Augustus

A82

Invergary **3**

4

Braemar

A93

5

Spean Bridge Λ86 **6** Dalwhinnie

1

Blair Athol

Fort William

A9

9

Pitlochry

A94

A82

Tyndrum

Crianlarich A85

Perth

A84

A83

North West Scotland & Highlands

01 **Corrour & Loch Ossian**

15km

Introduction

Set in the middle of Rannoch Moor, Loch Ossian is one of Scotland's highest lochs at almost 400m above sea level. At its eastern tip, Corrour Lodge dates back to the early 19th century and until the tracks which form this route were built, the lodge could only be reached by a combination of railway, pony and boat along the Loch. This is a simple, easy route with no technical difficulties. It's the stunning scenery and sense of wilderness which are the big attractions. This is a popular 'adventure' for families, due to the fact that the start of the route can only be accessed by rail, and the trip can be combined with an overnight stay at Loch Ossian Youth Hostel on the western shore of the Loch.

The Ride

Corrour Station is about a 45 minute train ride from Fort William. Bikes travel free, but should be booked in advance. The view from the station platform out over the empty wilderness of Rannoch Moor is impressive and really sets the tone for the ride. The route heads east from the station towards Loch Ossian Youth Hostel which overlooks the islands in the loch. The views towards Ben Alder and Aonach Beag beyond the loch are amazing. Carrying on along the south bank of the loch gives easy riding through the mixed woodland to Corrour Lodge – recently refurbished in an ultra-modern style, in contrast to the wild surroundings. Returning along the north side of the loch gives more stunning scenery and easy trails.

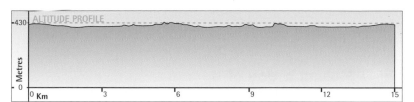

| CORROUR & LOCH OSSIAN | GRADE: ▲ |

TOTAL DISTANCE: 15KM » **TOTAL ASCENT**: 180M » **TIME**: 2–3 HOURS » **START/FINISH**: CORROUR RAILWAY STATION
START GRID REF: NN 356664 » **SATNAV**: PH33 6TQ (FORT WILLIAM STATION) » **OS MAP**: LANDRANGER 41 AND 42
ESTATE CONTACT: CORROUR ESTATE OFFICE TEL: 01397 732 200 » **YOUTH HOSTEL**: LOCH OSSIAN TEL: 01397 732 207
FIRST SCOTRAIL: TEL: 08457 550 033 » **CAFE**: CORROUR STATION HOUSE

Directions – Corrour & Loch Ossian

⊙→ From Corrour Station pick up the Landrover track that heads east towards Loch Ossian Youth Hostel.

2 After 1.4km the track splits: fork **R** to pass the Youth Hostel after another 400m. Carry on along the southern side of Loch Ossian to Corrour Lodge at the eastern end of the Loch.

3 Cross the bridge over the River Ossian and turn **L** at the junction, following the track along the north shore of the loch back towards Corrour.

4 At the junction, turn **R** to return to the railway station (or **L** if you intend to spend the night at the Youth Hostel).

←☉━ Making a day of it

Epic rides can be started from Corrour Station: taking the train from Fort William and riding back gives a good full day ride. Follow the Landrover track towards Loch Ossian initially, but turn northwest towards Loch Treig, then take the boggy track to Meannach bothy. From Meannach, the ascent of the Lairig Leacach involves some serious carrying, but the descent to the bothy is incredible. Then it's a matter of taking forest trails through Leanachan Forest to Nevis Range. If you have the energy you can fit in a lap of the 2007 World Mountain Bike Championship course, before taking the gentle tarmac cycle route back into Fort William. Pick up OS Landranger Map 41.

01 CORROUR & LOCH OSSIAN

© CROWN COPYRIGHT AND/OR DATABASE RIGHT. ALL RIGHTS RESERVED. LICENCE NUMBER 100025218.

02 **Loch Affric Loop**

Introduction

Glen Affric is said to be one of Scotland's most picturesque glens. On a crisp day, with the autumn leaves turning the trees a multitude of colours and the loch calm and clear, it's hard to argue with that statement. This ride takes a tour of Loch Affric using well-maintained tracks on the North Affric estate and returning on some superb undulating singletrack. Given the remote and wild environment, it's hard to believe that, before the Highland Clearances, this was a well populated glen. Currently, efforts are being made to return the woodland to a more natural state, restoring habitats for wildlife and providing future generations with a glimpse of Scotland from a previous era.

The Ride

From the village of Cannich, a winding single lane road ends with the Forestry Commission car park at the eastern end of Loch Affric. A well-surfaced estate track leads over a bridge and heads west through the beautiful woodland, giving glimpses of the impressive Affric Lodge on the opposite bank. At Athnamulloch the track becomes rockier as it passes abandoned buildings and crosses the Allt na Ciche. The rocky singletrack back along the north side of Loch Affric constantly climbs and descends, providing a challenge for beginners and a thrill for the more experienced. Several river crossings mean that there will be wet feet at the finish of this scenic ride.

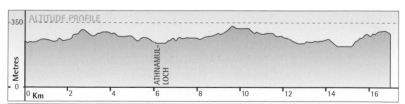

LOCH AFFRIC LOOP   **GRADE:** ▲

DISTANCE: 17KM » **TOTAL ASCENT**: 400M » **TIME**: 2–3 HOURS » **START/FINISH**: CAR PARK, LOCH AFFRIC
START GRID REF: NH 201234 » **SATNAV**: CANNICH » **OS MAP**: LANDRANGER 25 » **CONTACT**: AFFRIC LODGE
TEL: 01456 415 351 » **CAFÉ**: BOG COTTON CAFÉ, CANNICH CARAVAN PARK TEL: 01456 415 364

© CROWN COPYRIGHT AND/OR DATABASE RIGHT. ALL RIGHTS RESERVED. LICENCE NUMBER 100025218.

02 LOCH AFFRIC LOOP

Directions – Loch Affric Loop

5 From the car park, cross the bridge over the loch. Follow the Landrover track and take the **R** fork, approx 200m after the bridge. Follow this track through the woods along the south side of Loch Affric.

2 At the junction at Athnamulloch, go **R** onto the rocky track past the abandoned buildings and cross the Allt na Ciche on the metal bridge.

3 Turn **R** onto the narrower trail that climbs towards Loch Coulavie. This trail constantly climbs and descends above the loch as it makes its way back to Affric Lodge. The surface is loose and rocky and may be challenging in places for beginners. There are several burns to ford along the track. The crossing of the Allt Coulavie (GR NH 136220) can be difficult after heavy rain, but the others shouldn't offer any problems beyond wet feet!

4 The singletrack trail runs parallel with a fence and joins the main access track to Affric Lodge. Turn **L** and follow the access track back to the start.

◄⊙⊙ **Making a day of it**

It's possible to extend this route further west towards Allt Beithe. Packing supplies and a sleeping bag and spending the night at the remote and spectacular Glen Affric Youth Hostel is a great overnight trip. (Scottish Youth Hostels Association **www.syha.org.uk** Tel: **0870 155 3255**)

Also of note: The forest between Dog Falls on the road from Cannich, and Plodda Falls has single-track trails that are not marked on the map, but are definitely worth exploring.

03 **The Corrieyairack Pass**   36km

Introduction

The Corrieyairack Pass was built in the 1730s by General Wade as a route to ferry troops from Fort Augustus to the barracks at Ruthven. Nearly 300 years later, it has become one of the classic challenges of Scottish mountain biking. While not particularly technical, climbing from the tip of Loch Ness just 20m above sea level to almost 770m in one long unrelenting push, this is a challenging high mountain ride that will test fitness and determination to the limits. From the summit of the pass the loose and broken descent follows the infant River Spey as it begins its 107 mile journey across the country to the sea. Ending the ride at Laggan Wolftrax allows you to sample some of Scotland's best purpose-built mountain bike trails – if you have any energy left!

The Ride

This is a point-to-point route that will require two vehicles, as there are no public transport links between the start and finish points. From Fort Augustus the route skirts the southern end of Loch Ness before taking a narrow tree-lined road towards Glen Tarff. Shortly after crossing over the River Tarff the tarmac is left behind and climbing begins in earnest. There's no respite for the next 13km until the summit of the pass is reached. Over the top a cracking descent ensues, but the famous Corrieyairack hairpins have been washed away in places, leaving large boulders to clamber over. At Melgarve the track begins to run alongside the Spey, crossing farmland and dropping through the woods to Wolftrax.

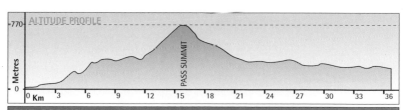

ALTITUDE PROFILE — 770 ... 0 — Metres — PASS SUMMIT — Km: 0 3 6 9 12 15 18 21 24 27 30 33 36

THE CORRIEYAIRACK PASS   **GRADE:** ▲

TOTAL DISTANCE: 36KM » **TOTAL ASCENT**: 1150M » **TIME**: 3-5 HOURS » **START**: FORT AUGUSTUS CAR PARK
START GRID REF: NH 378094 » **START SATNAV**: FORT AUGUSTUS » **FINISH**: LAGGAN WOLFTRAX
FINISH GRID REF: NN 593924 » **FINISH SATNAV**: PH20 1BU » **OS MAP**: LANDRANGER 34 AND 35 » **CAFE**: BASECAMP CAFÉ, WOLFTRAX TEL: 01528 544 786

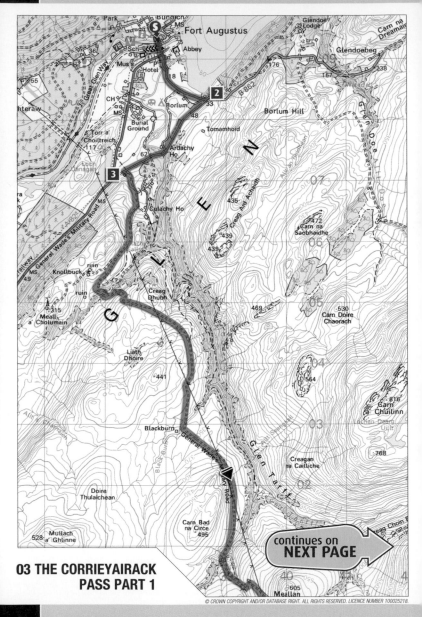

continues on
NEXT PAGE

03 THE CORRIEYAIRACK
PASS PART 1

© CROWN COPYRIGHT AND/OR DATABASE RIGHT. ALL RIGHTS RESERVED. LICENCE NUMBER 100025218.

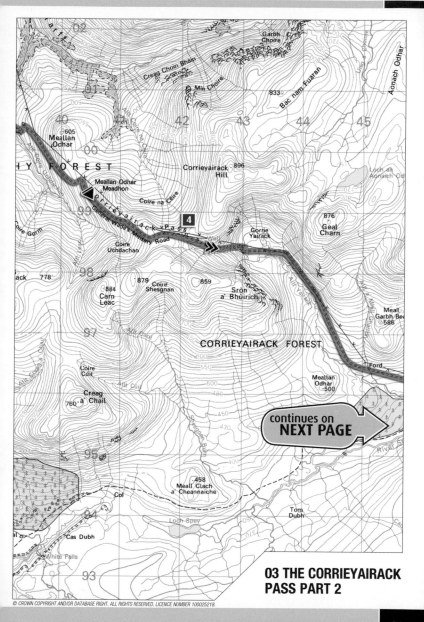

**continues on
NEXT PAGE**

**03 THE CORRIEYAIRACK
PASS PART 2**

© CROWN COPYRIGHT AND/OR DATABASE RIGHT. ALL RIGHTS RESERVED. LICENCE NUMBER 100025218.

© CROWN COPYRIGHT AND/OR DATABASE RIGHT. ALL RIGHTS RESERVED. LICENCE NUMBER 100025218.

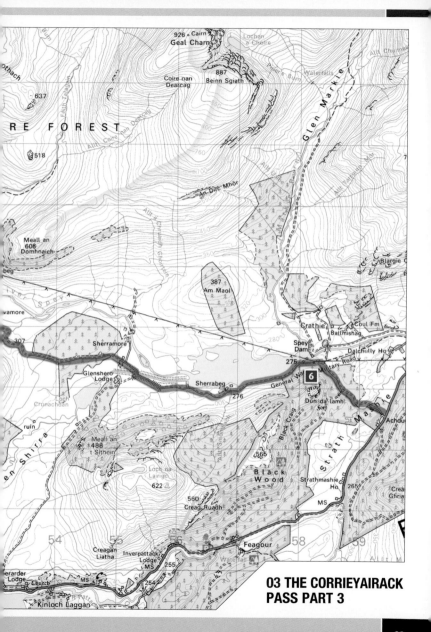

Directions – The Corrieyairack Pass

❺➤ From the large car park beside the Tourist Information Centre in Fort Augustus, cross the Caledonian Canal and take Glendoe Road (B862) along the south bank of Loch Ness. Make sure to keep an eye out for the monster!

2 After 1.5km, turn **R** onto a single lane tarmac road. Follow this for 1.9km, crossing the bridge over the River Tarff and past Ardachy Lodge.

3 At the farmhouse turn **L** following the track uphill. This track climbs up Glen Tarff and through Culachy Forest for 13km to the summit of the pass. It roughly follows a line of electricity pylons which continue the whole way to Laggan and beyond. The climb is well surfaced and the gradient always manageable, but it goes on for a very long time. It's a real test of willpower to get to the top without getting off and pushing.

4 From the summit of the pass the views are outstanding and the zig-zag descent is loose and rough. The surface has been completely washed away in places, which unfortunately interrupts the descent. The track improves as it reaches Melgarve and several of the original General Wade bridges can be seen along the way, before the track turns to tarmac near Garva Bridge.

5 From Garva Bridge follow the road for 7.3km through the farm at Sherramore and past the Spey Dam.

6 Take the forest track that leads off to the **R** just as the road passes under the power lines. Follow this for 1.75km to the car park at Laggan Woftrax.

04 Glengarry Forest Circuit 32km

Introduction

Glengarry Forest sits above Loch Lochy to the west of the Great Glen, the huge 400 million year old fault line that runs from Fort William to Inverness. This loop takes in part of the Great Glen Cycle Route along the shores of Loch Lochy, and climbs on smooth forest roads. It finishes with a fantastic descent through the Cam Bealach on an old coffin road which, in times gone by, crofters would have used to carry their dead to the church at Kilfinnan. This is another tough route with a prolonged climb to the high point meaning you really have to earn that final descent and a pint at the Eagle Inn – a barge floating on the Caledonian Canal!

The Ride

Starting at Laggan Locks, you must first cross the canal to pick up the minor road to North Laggan, which forms part of the Great Glen Cycle Route (Sustrans Route 78). This climbs through the woods above Loch Oich before swinging west just before the village of Invergarry. From Wester Mandally the trail climbs, steeply at first, on forest roads towards the Allt Ladaidh and Laddie Wood. On reaching the river, some tough trails lead out of the trees and past Lochan Fhudair into the Cam Bealach. The descent back towards Loch Lochy is superb. The old coffin road drops 500m in just over 3km of narrow rocky technical trails, before bursting out onto the smooth forest road past Kilfinnan and back to the start.

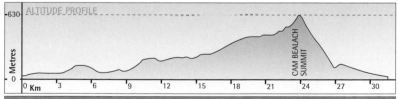

ALTITUDE PROFILE

630

Metres

0

0 Km   3   6   9   12   15   18   21   24   27   30

CAM BEALACH SUMMIT

GLENGARRY FOREST CIRCUIT   GRADE: ▲

DISTANCE: 32KM » **TOTAL ASCENT**: 950M » **TIME**: 3–4 HOURS » **START**: LAGGAN LOCKS CAR PARK
START GRID REF: NN 286962 » **SATNAV**: LAGGAN » **OS MAP**: LANDRANGER 34 » **PUB**: THE EAGLE INN, LAGGAN LOCKS
TEL: 07789 858 567

© CROWN COPYRIGHT AND/OR DATABASE RIGHT. ALL RIGHTS RESERVED. LICENCE NUMBER 100025218.

04 GLENGARRY FOREST CIRCUIT

Directions – Glengarry Forest Circuit

1 From the car park at Laggan Locks cross the canal and ride for 400m to meet the minor road to Kilfinnan. Turn **R** and follow the road to the junction with the A82.

2 Pick up the Great Glen Cycle Route (Sustrans Route 78), following it through the pine forest to Easter Mandally.

3 Follow the road through Wester Mandally, crossing the cattle grid at the end of the road and passing the gatehouse.

4 Cross the bridge and turn **L**. Follow the forest road for 5.5km along the side of the river and past several waterfalls to the Laddie Hut.

5 At the hut, which dates back to the 1880s, turn **L** onto the forest road that follows the Allt Ladaidh upstream for 2.1km.

6 Turn **R** onto the trail that traverses the lower slopes of Meall a' Choire Ghlais before climbing steeply to the high point of the route at the summit of the Cam Bealach.

7 From the summit, enjoy the fantastic technical descent which follows the Allt Glas Dhoire back into South Laggan Forest.

8 At the junction with the main forest road, turn **L** towards Kilfinnan. Pass the ancient graveyard, which has a mausoleum to the MacDonnells, one of the Clans of Invergarry. 1km after the graveyard turn **R** back to the start at Laggan Locks.

Introduction

The magnificent Ardverikie House, on
the banks of Loch Laggan, is instantly
recognisable as the estate house used in
the BBC's Monarch of the Glen television
series. It dates from the 1870s and was a
favourite destination of Queen Victoria.
This is a ride that takes you deep into
one of Scotland's oldest deer forests
and along the banks of Loch Laggan,
whose shores form the country's largest
freshwater beach. It is a ride of two
halves, the first climbing steadily to Loch
Pattack, before the steep ascent to the
north east ridge of Beinn a Chlachair.
The second half descends to Lochan na
h-Earba and Loch Laggan. The scenery
is spectacular and the terrain diverse on
this wonderful wilderness journey.

The Ride

The spectacular baronial style gatehouse
at the eastern end of Loch Laggan gives an
idea of the grandeur of the main Ardverikie
House at the very beginning of the ride.
From the gatehouse a good track leads
to the River Pattack and climbs gently
upstream past waterfalls and woodland.
Nearing Loch Pattack the views towards
Ben Alder are outstanding. From the loch,
the real climbing begins with a tough
ascent to the high point of the route above
Loch a Bhealaich Leamhain. The climbing
is instantly rewarded with the fantastic
descent to Lochan na h-Earba. From the
Lochan, gentle tracks along the shore lead
to Ardverikie House and some sandy riding
on the beach at Loch Laggan.

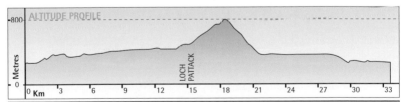

THE ARDVERIKIE ESTATE | GRADE: ▲

TOTAL DISTANCE: 34KM » **TOTAL ASCENT**: 850M » **TIME**: 3–5 HOURS » **START**: ARDVERIKIE ESTATE GATE HOUSE
START GRID REF: NN 539897 » **SATNAV**: KINLOCH LAGGAN » **OS MAP**: LANDRANGER 42 » **CONTACT**: ARDVERIKIE
ESTATE OFFICE TEL: 01528 544 300 » **CAFÉ**: BASECAMP CAFÉ, WOLFTRAX TEL: 01528 544 786

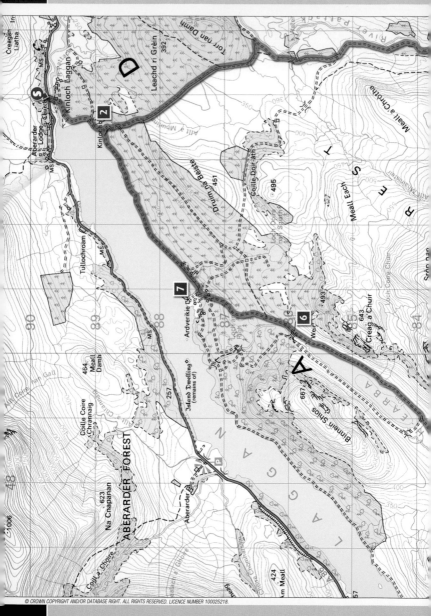

© CROWN COPYRIGHT AND/OR DATABASE RIGHT. ALL RIGHTS RESERVED. LICENCE NUMBER 100025218.

p85 Ben Alder

05 THE ARDVERIKIE ESTATE

Directions – The Ardverikie Estate

➊ The nearest official parking area to the start point is approximately 3km east on the A86 (Grid Ref: NN 566903). However, on the road there are several lay-bys closer to the start where a car can be parked, as well as the old filling station around 1km to the west. Cross the River Pattack using the bridge at the Ardverikie Estate gatehouse and follow this track towards Loch Laggan for just over 1km.

➋ Turn **L** at the track junction and follow the well-surfaced Landrover track along the edge of the woods towards the River Pattack. Follow the river upstream towards Loch Pattack. At the northern end of the Loch pass the two gateposts that stand alone and continue to the track junction approximately 800m further on.

➌ Turn **R** at the junction and follow the track along the south shore of Loch Pattack. The track can be submerged if the loch is high and it may be more sensible to use the suspension bridge to cross the Allt a Chaoil-reidhe as it empties into the loch, rather than attempting to ride through the river.

➍ At the junction at the western end of the loch carry on west, ignoring a track to the left (south). Ford the Allt Cam after 1.3km (plenty of stepping stones) and begin serious climbing for 3.25 km above the south side of Loch a Bhealaich Leamhain. This is a serious ascent and involves some hike-a-bike. The view from the high point on the east ridge of Beinn a Chlachair is quite spectacular though, and the singletrack descent down to Lochan na h-Earba is ample reward.

➎ Pick up the Landrover track along the eastern shore of Lochan a h-Earba. The new road which has been built along the loch makes for good going as the old road, which can still be seen closer to the waters edge, was very prone to flooding.

➏ At the bridge just past the head of the loch, continue **SA** for about 1.7km towards Ardverikie House.

➐ Turn **R** and follow the track along the sandy shores of Loch Laggan and back to the Ardverikie gatehouse.

A weekend away

This route runs very close to route no 6, Ben Alder (page 85). Loading up a bike trailer with food and camping gear and riding in to Culra bothy (NN 523762) from either Dalwhinnie (15.5km) or Kinloch Laggan (16.5km) means you can ride both routes over a weekend, with a fantastic overnight bothy stop.

06 Ben Alder

Introduction

A fantastic big-mountain day, in the heart of the Highlands. The village of Dalwhinnie, just off the A9, is famous for its whisky. The distillery, which dates from 1897, is open for tours and is definitely worth a look if you've any energy left at the end of a long day in the saddle. The ride departs from the village railway station, climbing to around 850 metres while circumnavigating the remote mountain of Ben Alder. The views from the high point of the route are simply breathtaking, and the terrain is some of the most enjoyable in Scotland. As well as fast flowing singletrack, there are cosy bothies, beautiful lochs and spectacular mountains all around. A tough, remote and testing day, but an incredible mountain bike ride.

The Ride

From Dalwhinnie the ride follows the bank of Loch Ericht into the mountains. A grassy trail leads to Culra bothy, before superb singletrack climbs into the Bealach Dubh. A short push gives access to the summit of the pass and wonderful views west to Strath Ossian. A fast, fun descent leads to the Bealach Cumhann. The path is narrow in places, leaving little margin for error if you overcook any of the turns at speed! The descent heads towards another bothy, the supposedly haunted Ben Alder Cottage. To avoid any supernatural encounters the route avoids the bothy with the toughest part of the day – a hike-a-bike section to the Bealach Breabag. It's well worth the effort for the fantastic technical descent back down to Culra. Then it's a simple matter of retracing the route back to Dalwhinnie.

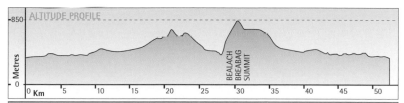

BEN ALDER	GRADE: ▲

DISTANCE: 53KM » **TOTAL ASCENT**: 1350M » **TIME**: 6–8 HOURS » **START/FINISH**: DALWHINNIE RAILWAY STATION
START GRID REF: NN 634849 » **SATNAV**: PH19 1AB » **OS MAP**: LANDRANGER 42 » **CONTACT**: BEN ALDER ESTATE
OFFICE TEL: 01528 522 253 » **PUB/CAFÉ**: THE INN, DAWHINNIE TEL: 01528 522 257 DALWHINNIE DISTILLERY VISITOR
CENTRE TEL: 01528 522 208

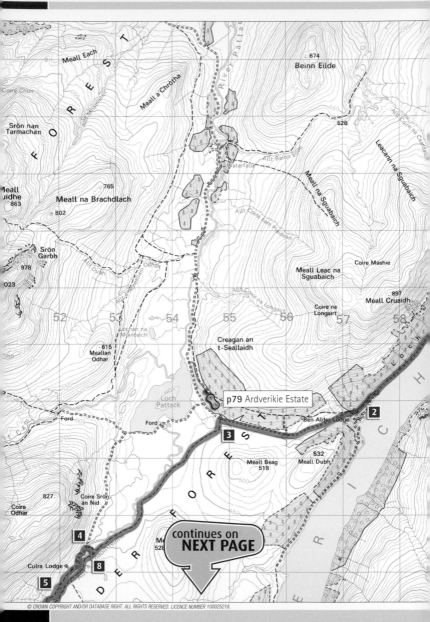

p79 Ardverikie Estate

continues on
NEXT PAGE

© CROWN COPYRIGHT AND/OR DATABASE RIGHT. ALL RIGHTS RESERVED. LICENCE NUMBER 100025218.

Directions – Ben Alder

➎ From Dalwhinnie railway station, use the level crossing at the southern end of the station to cross the tracks. Follow the Ben Alder Estate's access road along the side of Loch Ericht, south west towards Ben Alder Lodge.

2 At the fork, take the track to the **R**, which passes around the side of the main house in the direction of Loch Pattack.

3 After 3km, turn **L** onto a grassy vehicle track. This crosses open ground initially, then follows the south bank of the Allt a Chaoil-Reidhe.

4 Cross the rickety suspension bridge and turn **L** towards Culra bothy. This is an excellently appointed bothy and makes for a good spot to take a break.

5 Turn **L** onto the singletrack trail that branches off the main track and follows the river just upstream from the bothy. (Note: there are a number of stone drainage channels across the track. Make sure your bunnyhopping skills are honed, or risk pinch punctures.) The final 300m to the summit of the pass is very steep, loose and a carry is necessary.

6 On a clear day the view from the top of the pass to the west is quite stunning with Loch Ossian (see page 55 for Loch Ossian route) and the jagged peaks of the Mamores clearly visible. If the visibility is poor, the trail directly ahead may hold more interest. The gradient encourages high speeds and with the narrow track cut into the steep hillside, precise lines are needed to avoid going off the edge and down the slope! From the top of the pass, the descent drops around 450m towards Ben Alder Cottage, with only one small counter climb into the Bealach Cumhann along its 7km length.

7 Turn **L** up the steep singletrack climb that begins around 150m before Ben Alder Cottage. This is the toughest part of the day and involves a 2km hike-a-bike (with 450m ascent) to the summit of the Bealach Breabag. It's around an hour of hard work but its worth it when you see the trail which opens out below you – a 7km singletrack plummet through the Bealach Beithe, past the enormous Loch and back towards Culra. This is possibly one of the best descents in the country!

8 From the rickety bridge crossed earlier in the day, retrace the same route back towards Ben Alder Lodge and Dalwhinnie.

**06 BEN ALDER
PART 2**

© CROWN COPYRIGHT AND/OR DATABASE RIGHT. ALL RIGHTS RESERVED. LICENCE NUMBER 100025218.

07 **Glen Sligachan** – Isle of Skye   46km

Introduction

The Isle of Skye is famous the world over for the raw natural beauty of its landscape. Set in the shadows of the towering Cuillin Hills, this loop, taking in Glen Sligachan and Strath Mor, is a real classic. A ride where man and machine are put to the test against the island's wild, rugged terrain and notoriously hostile weather. Traditionally, this loop is ridden anti-clockwise, but it is described in the opposite direction here to avoid a long tarmac section with a nasty climb towards the finish. Although the distance, height gain and amount of tarmac make it look modest on paper, this ride is a real epic which will test even the fittest and most competent of mountain bikers.

The Ride

An hour of road riding from Sligachan allows for a good warm up along the shores of Loch Sligachan and Loch Ainort. At Luib the shift from tarmac to technical is abrupt with Strath Mor providing some great singletrack on the way to the head of Loch Slapin. After passing the fishing boats moored at Faoilean, the only real climb of the day begins. The first half is taken care of on tarmac, then on a loose rocky trail over Am Mam, before a fast, boulder-strewn descent back to sea level at Camasunary. The return to Sligachan is the highlight of the ride: 12km of the most relentless, challenging and, at times, downright punishing singletrack. This is a real test of fitness and handling skills and is a fitting finish to a true epic.

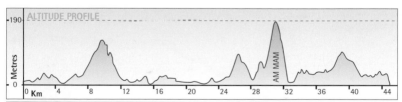

GLEN SLIGACHAN – ISLE OF SKYE   GRADE: ▲

DISTANCE: 46KM » **TOTAL ASCENT**: 1000M » **TIME**: 5-7 HOURS » **START/FINISH**: SLIGACHAN HOTEL
START GRID REF: NG 486299 » **SATNAV**: IV47 8SW » **OS MAP**: LANDRANGER 32 » **PUB**: SLIGACHAN HOTEL
TEL: 01478 650 204

© CROWN COPYRIGHT AND/OR DATABASE RIGHT. ALL RIGHTS RESERVED. LICENCE NUMBER 100025218.

07 GLEN SLIGACHAN – ISLE OF SKYE

Directions – Glen Sligachan – Isle of Skye

➲ From the parking area on the north side of the Sligachan Hotel, turn **R** along the main road (A87) heading east and then south for 16km. Taking the minor road around the coast via Moll adds about 3km to the overall distance, but has much less traffic than the main road.

2 At Luib turn **R** off the main road, after the bridge over the river. After approximately 400m take the second gate on the **L**, opposite the two cottages. Follow this track into Strath Mor. This singletrack trail is boggy and technical.

3 The path becomes indistinct along the shores of Lochain Stratha Mhoir. Once past the south end of the loch, the path improves on the opposite side of the river. It is easiest to continue on the west side until you get to the point where a section of the hillside has been washed out, leaving a rocky scree slope. Fording the river at this point and carrying on directly up the scree on the opposite bank for around 100 metres will bring you to the track. Follow this to the road at Clach Oscar, at the head of Loch Slapin. The path is very close to the edge of Loch na Sguabaidh and after heavy rain, when the loch is full, you will find yourself riding through the loch. Just make sure you keep pedalling as the water starts to lap around your top tube!

4 Turn **R** onto the single lane tarmac road and follow it towards Kirkibost. This section gives nice views of the fishing boats moored at Faoilean as well Bla Bheinn and the other Cuillins. After 3.5km the road turns inland and climbs towards Kirkibost.

5 Approximately 400m after the junction for Kilmarie, turn **R** and go through the gate at the signpost for Camasunary and Sligachan. Follow this track, which gets steeper and rockier as it climbs over the Am Mam pass and descends towards Camasunary.

6 Turn downhill on the steep rocky trail, crossing the river towards the abandoned buildings at Camasunary.

7 It should be hard to miss the turn off for Sligachan, as it is painted in large letters on the ruined cottage, with an equally big arrow pointing the way. This is the toughest and most challenging section of the ride. Apart from a few short, boggy sections it's rideable all the way back to Sligachan, but if your technical singletrack skills are having an off day you'll struggle!

08 **Torridon Circuit**

Introduction

The dramatic landscape of Wester Ross, where 750 million year old sandstone rises up out of the sea to form massive mountains, is the awe-inspiring backdrop to this superb mountain bike ride. Torridon village is remote and isolated, accessed only by a singletrack road which follows the river down the glen. It has long been a destination for mountaineers keen to scale the giants such as Liathach and Beinn Eighe, but it also has some superb trails hidden away in the remote glens. This stunning route takes in some of the best wilderness singletrack Scotland has to offer in some of the most spectacular landscapes you are likely to encounter anywhere. This is a tough and committing route, suitable for well prepared and experienced riders.

The Ride

From Glen Torridon, warm up and marvel at the scenery on the initial road section. At Loch Clair it's time to turn off the tarmac into the Coulin Forest. Given the rugged terrain all around, the climb up the Coulin Pass is surprisingly civilised: the track is well-surfaced, the gradient manageable – it just goes on for a long, long time! Your hard work is rewarded with amazing views down Strathcarron and a warp speed, forest road descent to Achnashellach. At Coulags the singletrack trail, which climbs to Loch Coire Fionnaraich, is narrow, rocky and flecked with pink sandstone. It's technical in places, boggy in others, but mostly rideable all the way to Bealach na Lice. The descent to Annat is one of the best you'll find anywhere. Gravelly singletrack flows past Lochs, over rock slabs and through burns in the shadow of some of the most spectacular mountains in Scotland.

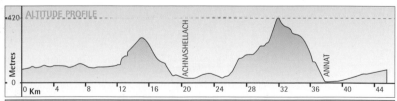

TORRIDON CIRCUIT   **GRADE:** ▲

DISTANCE: 46KM » **TOTAL ASCENT**: 1100M » **TIME**: 6-8 HOURS » **START/FINISH**: CAR PARK, GLEN TORRIDON
START GRID REF: NG 959569 » **SATNAV**: TORRIDON » **OS MAP**: LANDRANGER 25 » **CONTACT**: COULIN ESTATE
OFFICE 01445 760 383. ACHNASHELLACH ESTATE OFFICE 01520 766 266 » **PUB**: LOCH TORRIDON INN TEL: 01445 791 242

© CROWN COPYRIGHT AND/OR DATABASE RIGHT. ALL RIGHTS RESERVED. LICENCE NUMBER 100025218.

continues on
NEXT PAGE

**08 TORRIDON CIRCUIT
PART 1**

continues on PREVIOUS PAGE

© CROWN COPYRIGHT AND/OR DATABASE RIGHT. ALL RIGHTS RESERVED. LICENCE NUMBER 100025218.

**08 TORRIDON CIRCUIT
PART 2**

Directions – Torridon Circuit

⊙➤ From the car park, cross the metal bridge and follow the road east towards Kinlochewe.

2 After 5km turn **R** onto the track leading to Coulin Lodge.

3 At the lodge, continue **SA** through the gate. (Signposted *Footpath.*)

4 After 800m branch off onto a narrow singletrack trail which runs along the edge of Loch Coulin towards the cottage at Torran-cuilinn. This track is technical in places and at times disappears into the loch, but is rideable for most of its length.

5 At Torran-cuilinn turn **R** to cross the wooden bridge over the River Coulin, aiming for the lodge house on the edge of the forest.

6 At the lodge house at Coulin turn **L** and follow the track along the forest edge.

7 After 1.9km turn **L**, crossing the bridge over the River Coulin. Follow this track which has a good surface and a manageable gradient to the summit of the Coulin Pass, before entering the forest and descending towards Achnashellach Station. The forest road descent is smooth, open and very fast.

8 Go straight through the crossroads in the forest tracks to the level crossing. Very carefully cross the railway line and take the track to the main road. Turn **R** and continue along the main road for 6km to Coulags.

9 Pass the cottages at Coulags and turn **R** onto the track, signposted *Public Right of Way to Torridon.* After approx 200m branch off **L** onto the footpath, just before the cattle grid. Follow this track past the bothy towards Loch Coire Fionnraich.

10 Continue **SA** at a fork in the path, marked by a small cairn. The path becomes more challenging from this point, with a few short unrideable sections to Bealach na Lice.

11 At the Bealach, the path splits again at another small cairn. Go **L** to the summit of the pass and begin descending to the northern tip of Loch an Eion.

12 At the junction turn **R** towards the distinctively shaped Lochan Domhain. This amazing singletrack trail offers what must be one of the most fantastic descents in Scotland as it drops over 400m to sea level at Annat.

13 At Annat, turn **R** towards Torridon and follow the road back to the start.

09 **West Highlands Tour**

Introduction

Set amongst the jagged rocky peaks that characterise the western Highlands, this is a fantastic overnight expedition into the wilderness. Pack some light-weight camping gear in a bike trailer or rucksack, and head for Nevis Range. The route loops around Ben Nevis, the highest mountain in Britain, and the Mamore mountain range before striking out into the wild open space to the head of Glen Nevis. There's a great bothy to spend the night in before starting the second day with a high mountain pass among stunning surroundings. A wonderful singletrack descent leads to some gentle forest riding to finish. This is a route with all the elements of a superb mountain bike adventure.

The Ride

From Nevis Range, the route follows the cycle track towards Fort William before picking up the West Highland Way on the outskirts of the town. Climbing through Nevis Forest the track runs along an old military road and past long abandoned settlements to Mamore Lodge Hotel. Past the hotel, the twin lochs of Loch Eilde Mor and Loch Eilde Beag guide the way to the open wilderness bound by Loch Treig and the Grey Corries. Meannanach bothy is a splendid place to spend the night, before tackling the climb of the Lairig Leacach on the second day. The descent back to Leanachan Forest is the high point of the trip before forest roads lead back to Nevis Range.

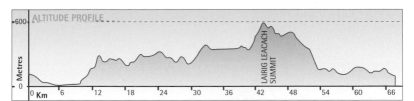

WEST HIGHLANDS TOUR   GRADE: ▲

DISTANCE: 69KM » **TOTAL ASCENT**: 1700M (APPROX) » **TIME**: 2 DAYS (4–6 HOURS PER DAY) » **START/FINISH**: NEVIS RANGE » **START GRID REF**: NN 171774 » **START SATNAV**: PH33 6SW » **OS MAP**: LANDRANGER 41
ESTATE CONTACT: MAMORE ESTATE TEL: 01855 831 337 » **CAFÉ**: NEVIS RANGE TEL: 01397 705 825

continues on
NEXT PAGE

© CROWN COPYRIGHT AND/OR DATABASE RIGHT. ALL RIGHTS RESERVED. LICENCE NUMBER 100025218.

**09 WEST HIGHLANDS
TOUR PART 1**

© CROWN COPYRIGHT AND/OR DATABASE RIGHT. ALL RIGHTS RESERVED. LICENCE NUMBER 100025218.

continues on **PREVIOUS PAGE**

09 WEST HIGHLANDS TOUR PART 2

Directions – West Highlands Tour

➏ From the car park at Nevis Range, ride back along the main access road for 700m and turn **L** onto the old tarmac road to Torlundy. Where this joins the A82 turn **L** and pick up the cycle track which runs alongside the main road back towards Fort William.

2 At the junction with the A830 leave the cycle track and ride **SA** along the road for 1.9km to the roundabout at the Nevis Bridge, turn **L** into Glen Nevis.

3 After 2.3km turn **R** onto the track marked as part of the West Highland Way. Follow the markers through Nevis Forest towards the southern slopes of the Mamores. After 13km pass the ruins of cottages at Larigmor and 1.5km later at Tigh na Sleubhaich, before descending towards Kinlochleven.

4 At the track junction, leave the West Highland Way, taking the Landrover track contouring round the hillside, passing the radio mast station on its way to Mamore Lodge Hotel.

5 Pass the impressive hotel building and follow the track as it climbs away from the hotel to cross the Allt Coire na Ba, 1km after the hotel.

6 Continue climbing towards Loch Eilde Mor, before dropping down to pass the disused boathouse at the western end of the loch.

7 From the boathouse, 7.5km of relatively flat and well surfaced Landrover track runs past the twin lochs of Loch Eilde Mor and Loch Eilde Beag to Luibeilt.

8 At Luibeilt the Abhainn Rath must be crossed. This river can carry a very large volume of water and may be impassable after heavy rainfall. **Meannanach bothy on the north side of the river is the perfect spot to spend the night if you're splitting the route over two days. It's large and well appointed and the views and location are simply wonderful.**

9 From Meannanach, the next 2.5km make up the testing climb up into the Lairig Leacach. The start of the climb is difficult to find. It is easiest to follow the river upstream for 300m from the bothy and pick up the path which is on a small ridge. If you pass the collapsed stone walls of old buildings you are slightly too far west, but

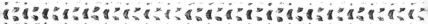

turning back and clambering up the rise will bring you to the path. **(Note: The climb to the summit will involve a lot of hike-a-bike, which can be hard work, especially if you have opted to tow your overnight gear in a trailer.)**

10 From the small cairn, which marks the summit of the pass, descend for 3km to the Lairig Leacach Bothy. This narrow, rocky singletrack descent down to the bothy is superb and the rugged surroundings make this section the highlight of the trip.

11 The Lairig Leacach bothy, sitting beneath Stob Ban, is tiny compared to Meannanach, but is still a fine place to stop for the night if you have made good progress on the first day, or just want to take a breather on the second day. From the bothy, a well-surfaced Landrover track climbs for just over 1km as it follows the Allt na Lairige upstream to the watershed. The next 7km are a fast and open descent towards Spean Bridge and the eastern end of Leanachan Forest.

12 At the track junction turn **L** and enter the forest following the forest track for 2.5km to the next junction.

13 Turn **R** at the junction. Follow the track for 2.5km crossing two rivers.

14 1km after the second bridge, turn **L**. Continue along this track, crossing the tarmac access road to Leanachan after 3.25km to the track junction after a further 1.1km.

15 Turn **R** and follow the forest track for 4.75km back to Nevis Range.

MEANNANACH BOTHY PHOTO: PHIL MCKANE

SECTION 3

North East Scotland & Cairngorms

Open a road map to this part of Scotland and the one thing you won't find is many roads. This is wild and untamed land, home to the Cairngorm Mountains, which provide a stunning backdrop to this selection of superb, wilderness rides.

North East Scotland & Cairngorms

sponsored by **GORE**
BIKE WEAR™

www.gorebikewear.com

UATH LOCHAN, GLEN FESHIE

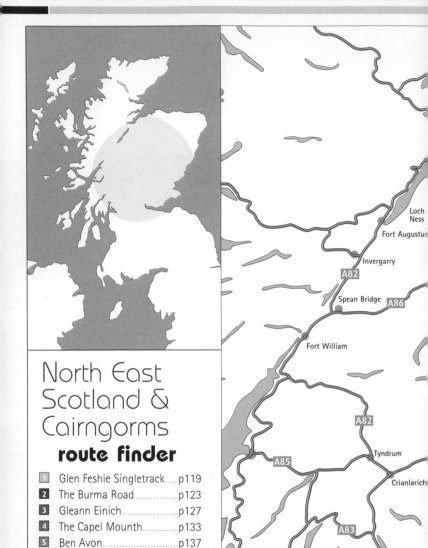

North East
Scotland &
Cairngorms
route finder

Loch
Ness

Fort Augustus

Invergarry

A82

Spean Bridge   A86

Fort William

A82

Tyndrum

A85

Crianlarich

A83

A82

North East Scotland & Cairngorms

Glen Feshie Singletrack   16km

Introduction

Glen Feshie is undoubtedly one of Scotland's most idyllic spots with a meandering river, twisted weathered trees and towering peaks. It is also home to some of the most fantastic trails in the country. Right from the start, narrow singletrack peppered with rocks and roots cuts through the heather and provides fantastic, flowing riding. A challenging climb at the halfway point makes your legs work, but the following descent more than makes up for it! This is a superb short ride, guaranteed to put a smile on the face of any singletrack fan.

The Ride

From the start the first section of singletrack comes after less than one kilometre. The trail follows the River Feshie, at first through the heather on the open moor, then into the woods before picking up an old vehicle track to the bridge at Carnachuin. Crossing this rickety old bridge is always entertaining, especially if you watch the planks jumping about as riders rattle over them! Next comes the main challenge of the day in the form of a steep, loose climb. At the top it's back into the trees for a fantastic singletrack descent down to Corarnstilmore, where gently rolling forest tracks lead back towards the River Feshie. Cross via another bridge and reverse the initial singletrack for a superb finish.

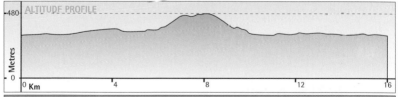

GLEN FESHIE SINGLETRACK   **GRADE:** ▲

TOTAL DISTANCE: 16KM » **TOTAL ASCENT**: 330M » **TIME**: 1.5–2.5 HOURS » **START/FINISH**: CAR PARK, AUCHLEAN NEAR FESHIEBRIDGE » **START GRID REF**: NN 851985 » **SATNAV**: FESHIEBRIDGE » **OS MAP**: LANDRANGER 43 **CONTACT**: GLEN FESHIE ESTATE TEL: 01540 651 880 » **CAFÉ**: THE POTTING SHED, INSHRIACH NURSERY TEL 01540 651 287

Directions – Glen Feshie Singletrack

↦ From the car park, follow the road to the farm at Auchlean.

2 Pass the farm and pick up the singletrack which runs parallel to the river. There are several options here as the tracks branch and converge. These tracks are not well represented on the OS map, but aim to stay on the higher ground above the river, passing through the gate in the deer fence at Achleum.

3 Cross the Allt Garbhlach and follow the singletrack trail through the trees. This joins up with a wider vehicle track which follows the River to Carnachuin Bridge.

4 Cross the bridge and climb steeply to the tarmac estate road. Turn **R** and then **L** after 400m onto the stony track that climbs away from the road and up the hillside.

5 After 1.2km, just over the crest of the hill, turn **R** onto the lesser track that enters the trees. This section can be muddy and hard work in the wet.

6 The main track makes a sharp 90 degree turn to the left. Continue **SA** here, through an old gate with no fence and descend on fantastic singletrack to Corarnstilmore. Turn **R** and follow the forest road back towards the River Feshie.

7 Turn **R** onto the tarmac estate road. Follow this for 1.2km to the bridge. Cross the bridge and return to the gate in the deer fence. Follow the singletrack from the start of the ride in reverse, past the farm at Auchlean and back to the car park.

←◌◌ Making a day of it

Turning **L** before crossing Carnachuin Bridge gives a huge, but totally rideable climb to near the summit of Carn Ban Mor. The descent back into Glen Feshie drops 700m in 4.5km! It is wonderfully technical, rocky singletrack the whole way and the views from the top are stunning. This is a demanding ride in the high mountains for skilled and experienced riders. OS Landranger 43.

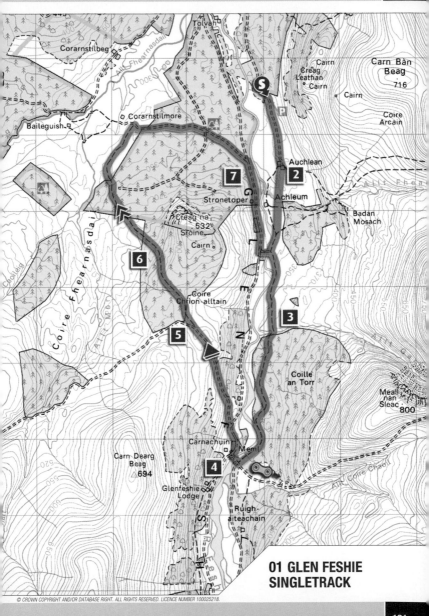

**01 GLEN FESHIE
SINGLETRACK**

© CROWN COPYRIGHT AND/OR DATABASE RIGHT. ALL RIGHTS RESERVED. LICENCE NUMBER 100025218.

02 **The Burma Road** 16km

Introduction

The Monadhliath or 'Grey Hills' are situated to the west of the Cairngorms. Their summits are lower and their terrain a little less rocky, but they provide excellent routes within easy reach of Aviemore. This route is a shortened version of the classic Burma Road circuit, squeezing a huge climb and superb descent into its short length. It climbs high into the hills, using the steep direct route to the saddle between Geal Charn Mor and Geal Charn Beag. From this high point, the route turns immediately back on itself, losing all that hard-won altitude in an adrenaline-fuelled descent. It's high-speed rocky singletrack that just seems to get steeper the further you descend. Although short, the unforgiving climb means this is a tough route, and it is the very definition of 'earning the descent'.

The Ride

Starting from Aviemore, the route follows the road out of town before turning towards Lynwilg. From here the climbing begins – a brutal granny ring grind which winches you straight up the mountainside to the 700m contour. The singletrack descent leads off from the cairn at the summit of the climb. Dropping over rocks and splashing through boggy streams as it drops on its ever steepening way back to the farm at Ballinluig. Passing under the main road and riding along the edge of Loch Alvie bring you back out to the road for the short return leg back to Aviemore.

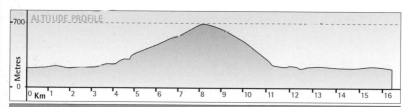

THE BURMA ROAD GRADE: ▲

TOTAL DISTANCE: 16KM » **TOTAL ASCENT**: 600M » **TIME**: 2–3 HOURS » **START/FINISH**: AVIEMORE TOWN CENTRE
START GRID REF: NH 895124 » **SATNAV**: AVIEMORE » **OS MAP**: LANDRANGER 35 » **CONTACT**: ALVIE ESTATE
TEL: 01540 651 255 » **CAFÉ**: CAFÉ MAMBO TEL: 01479 811 670

Directions – The Burma Road

➏ From Aviemore town centre follow the road south out of town. Go **SA** at the roundabout and after 1.8km turn **R** towards the main road, the A9.

2 **Cross the A9 extremely carefully**, taking the road directly opposite the junction. Pass the entrance to the first farm on the left.

3 Turn **L** into the track after crossing the Allt-na-Criche. Follow this well-defined track, with almost 5km of serious climbing, to the high point of the ride.

4 At the summit cairn take the track (south) that doubles back **L** almost exactly in the direction in which you have come. Drop your saddle and enjoy this excellent descent down to the farm at Ballinluig.

5 At the fork approximately 700m after the farm, turn **R**, pass under the A9 and follow the tarmac road along the edge of Loch Alvie to the road.

6 Turn **L** for approx. 3.5km of tarmac riding back to Aviemore.

←◉ **Making a day of it**

This is a shortened version of the full Burma Road circuit. To complete the full loop continue **SA** on from the cairn in the saddle at point 4 to cross the River Dulnain. Turn **R** just after the bridge and pass Caggan bothy, following the river to the old military road which now forms an off-road section of Sustrans Cycle Route 7. It's then a simple matter of following the Sustrans markers back to Aviemore via Sluggan and Carrbridge, although more adventurous alternatives are available through the surrounding woodland. Taking the loop in the anti-clockwise direction means you can finish on a high with the superb descent to Ballinluig. OS Landranger 35.

02 THE BURMA ROAD

© CROWN COPYRIGHT AND/OR DATABASE RIGHT. ALL RIGHTS RESERVED. LICENCE NUMBER 100025218.

ROTHIEMURCHUS
Glen Einich
take litter home
keep dogs under close

03 **Gleann Einich**

Introduction

Gleann Einich cuts a deep north-south trench into the eastern end of the Cairngorms and terminates with the beautiful Loch Einich, sandwiched between the slopes of Braeriach and Sgor Gaoith. This out-and-back ride starts by passing through the ancient Scots Pines in Rothiemurchus Forest before making its way deep into the mountains and the head of the loch. As an introduction to wilderness mountain biking in Scotland, Gleann Einich is perfect as it provides a real remote mountain feel without the difficulties of complex navigation or challenging terrain.

The Ride

The ride starts with a gentle warm-up on a newly constructed cycle path beside the road. On turning into Rothiemurchus the well-used paths make for easy cycling initially. After a crossroads in the forest, it becomes obvious that this is the road less travelled and the surface becomes looser with large rocks and roots on the trails. The track, surrounded by towering peaks, leads very gradually uphill. The surface is generally good, but there are river crossings and a few loose rocky sections to keep you on your toes. Eventually Loch Einich with its small sandy beach is reached. If the wind is funnelling down the glen turn around for a high speed, wind-assisted return leg!

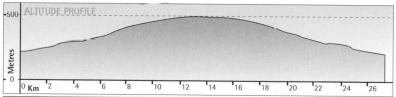

GLEANN EINICH   **GRADE:** ▲

DISTANCE: 28KM » **TOTAL ASCENT**: 470M » **TIME**: 2.5-4 HOURS » **START/FINISH**: BOTHY BIKES CAR PARK, INVERDRUIE
START GRID REF: NH 901110 » **SATNAV**: INVERDRUIE » **OS MAP**: LANDRANGER 36 » **CAFÉ**: ROTHIEMURCHUS VISITOR
CENTRE TEL: 01479 812 345 » **PUB**: THE OLD BRIDGE INN, AVIEMORE TEL: 01479 811 137 » **BIKE SHOP**: BOTHY BIKES
TEL: 01479 810 111

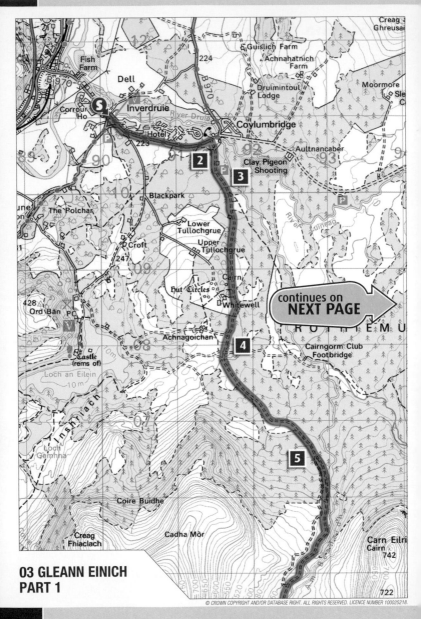

continues on NEXT PAGE

03 GLEANN EINICH
PART 1

© CROWN COPYRIGHT AND/OR DATABASE RIGHT. ALL RIGHTS RESERVED. LICENCE NUMBER 100025218.

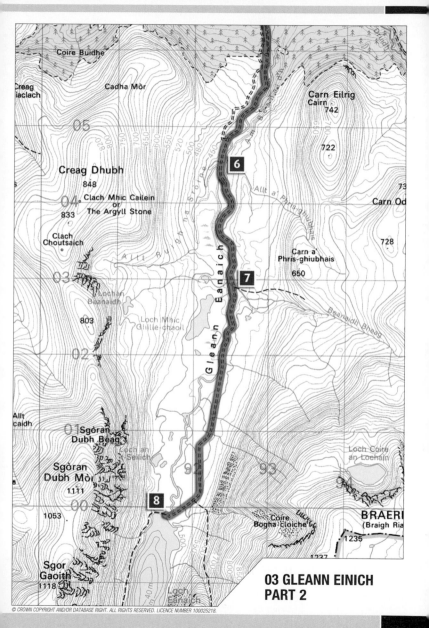

03 GLEANN EINICH
PART 2

© CROWN COPYRIGHT AND/OR DATABASE RIGHT. ALL RIGHTS RESERVED. LICENCE NUMBER 100025218.

Directions – Gleann Einich

6. From the Bothy Bikes car park in Inverdruie, follow the cycle track uphill towards Coylumbridge.

2 Turn **R** into the forest at Coylumbridge Caravan / Camp Site. Follow the track along the edge of the campsite and through a gate. Rothiemurchus is popular with walkers and families so bear this in mind on these trails.

3 At the fork turn **R**. Pass through several deer gates on this section.

4 The track comes to a crossroads with another track leading to either Loch An Eilean or the Cairngorm Club footbridge. Continue **SA** and pass through a gate. At this point the track becomes rougher and looser.

5 At the junction take the **L** trail which is narrower and stays close to the river.

6 Cross the river using either the metal footbridge or the ford to its left.

7 Follow the track to the head of Loch Einich. There are three water crossings on this section. The crossing of the Beanaidh Beag has stepping stones at the downstream edge of the track.

8 Loch Einich. Find somewhere to shelter from the ever present wind, enjoy a snack and reverse the route back to the start.

◄◎◎ Making a day of it

Rothiemurchus Forest is littered with trails that are perfect for riding. Bothy Bikes sells maps which mark out all the best singletrack. There are literally miles of trails to explore!

04 **The Capel Mounth**

24km

Introduction

The Capel Mounth is a remote challenging ride on an ancient trade route connecting Deeside and Angus. The first climb is tough with some hike-a-bike before the gradient eases. The Capel Mounth itself climbs on a well surfaced track, but its length and steep pitches are real leg breakers! The scenery and terrific descents make all the climbing worth it: The first downhill is so steep you think you may free fall to the bottom if you overshoot a bend! The best is saved until last though, as the final drop to the finish is on a narrow ribbon of rocky singletrack which has been described as one of the best descents in Scotland.

The Ride

Starting in Glen Doll, the route first follows the River South Esk before steep singletrack winds its way up to the plateau above Corrie Chash. Rocky tracks above Lock Muick (pronounced 'Mick') lead to a very steep descent over water bars and round rocky hairpins to cross the Black Burn. The trail follows the loch sides to the second big climb, over the Capel Mounth itself. A signpost points the way just before the Spittal of Glen Muick. After a long and energy sapping climb, the best bit of the ride is saved for last with the final descent back into Glen Doll. This is a wonderfully tight, twisty, rocky singletrack descent, first through the heather of the open hillside, and then on a ribbon of dirt that splashes through the Capel Burn in Glen Doll forest.

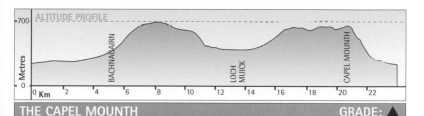

THE CAPEL MOUNTH   **GRADE:** ▲

DISTANCE: 24KM » **TOTAL ASCENT:** 1000M » **TIME:** 3-5 HOURS » **START/FINISH:** FORESTY COMMISSION CAR PARK, GLEN DOLL » **START GRID REF:** NO 284761 » **SATNAV:** KIRRIEMUIR/CLOVA » **OS MAP:** LANDRANGER 44 » **CONTACT:** HOUSE OF GLENMUICK TEL: 01339 755 427 » **CAFÉ:** NONE ON ROUTE » **PUB:** GLEN CLOVA HOTEL TEL: 01575 550 350

Directions – The Capel Mounth

① From the Forestry Commission car park, go back across the bridge and turn **L** onto the forest track.

2 Follow the track around the right (east) side of the farmhouse at Moulzie. The map shows a track going through the small wood, but follow the wooden boardwalk just before the trees to a singletrack trail which skirts the east side of the river.

3 Cross the river on the wooden bridge and follow the track up the glen into the woods at Bachnagairn. Approaching the trees the track becomes very rocky and difficult to ride and you'll be off and pushing before entering the woods.

4 Cross the wooden bridge over the small waterfall and begin climbing. This track is unrideable at first, but the gradient eases and the rock steps disappear nearer the top and it becomes a good singletrack climb.

5 Turn **R** at the track junction, pass the hut with Sanny's Seat and carry on along this track ignoring all other junctions. Descend to the bridge over Black Burn. Take care on the loose rocky hairpin corners and concrete water bars crossing the track.

6 Turn **R** at the junction signposted *Public Footpath to Glen Clova via Capel Mounth*. Follow this track ignoring the two junctions to the left. From the top of Capel Mounth follow fast rocky singletrack on the open hillside before entering the forest and crossing Capel Burn.

7 Turn **L** at the junction with forest track and return to the car park.

04 THE CAPEL MOUNTH

© CROWN COPYRIGHT AND/OR DATABASE RIGHT. ALL RIGHTS RESERVED. LICENCE NUMBER 100025218.

05 **Ben Avon**   68km

Introduction

Ben Avon, the most easterly of the Cairngorm mountains, is instantly recognisable due to its granite tors which jut from the summit plateau. A remote and inaccessible mountain, it provides the perfect setting for this, the epitome of the Scottish epic. Make no mistake, at almost 70km, with nearly 2000m of climbing and a big hike-a-bike section, this ride is a monster! For mere mortals, Faindouran bothy sits at almost exactly the half-way point. Carrying some basic camping gear means the ride can be split over two days, with an idyllic overnight stop in the heart of the mountains. However you attempt it, this is a challenging ride in difficult terrain and is best saved for the long days of summer.

The Ride

Starting at Linn of Dee gets the tarmac covered early on, although if you plan to split the route over two days, starting at Braemar divides the distance more evenly. Following the road through Braemar takes you across the River Dee at Invercauld Bridge, where you leave the tarmac heading towards the castle. Climbing above the pine forest and through the Bealach Dearg to Glen Builg brings some great lochside singletrack. At the Linn of Avon, the track follows the deep glen to Faindouran Lodge. Here the hard work starts to reach the Lairig an Laoigh – the Pass of the Calves. This ancient cattle drovers' route heads south in the shadow of the Cairngorms' highest summits to a singletrack finale in Glen Derry.

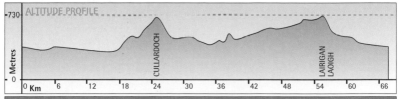

BEN AVON   **GRADE:** ▲

DISTANCE: 68KM » **TOTAL ASCENT**: 1900M » **TIME**: 7–10 HOURS » **START/FINISH**: LINN OF DEE CAR PARK
START GRID REF: NO 063898 » **SATNAV**: BRAEMAR » **OS MAP**: LANDRANGER 36 AND 43 » **ESTATE CONTACT**: MAR LODGE TEL: 01339 741 433 » **PUB**: FIFE ARMS HOTEL, BRAEMAR TEL: 01339 741 644

© CROWN COPYRIGHT AND/OR DATABASE RIGHT. ALL RIGHTS RESERVED. LICENCE NUMBER 100025218.

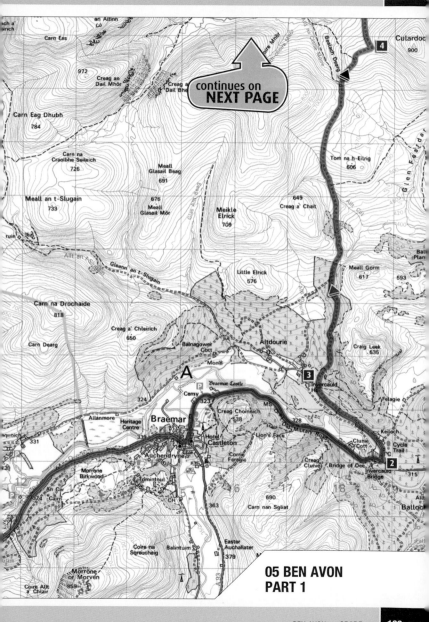

continues on
NEXT PAGE

**05 BEN AVON
PART 1**

Carn Dubh

818

Coire
Odhar

730

73

Mona
nan B

08

Bynack
Beg
964

Bynack
More
1090

Barns of
Bynack

A' Choinneach
1017

Lochan
a' Bhainne

748

742

Cnap an
Dòbhrain
694

Crapan a'
Mheirlich
680

07

G L E N

8

Faindouran
Lodge

Dagrum
848

Creag Mhòr
895

797

N

A

06

F O R E S T

05

Meall
Tional
799

04

Spion Rocks

Cnap Leum
an Easaich
917

Fords of Avon
Refuge

9

Stepping
Stones

Dubh
Lochan

Coire nan
Clach

CAIRNGORMS NATIONAL PARK

03

Coire
Ruairidh

02

Beinn a'
Chaorainn Bheag
1017

892

1172

A

I

N

S

1082
Beinn a'
Chaorainn

North Top
1197

Cnap
Chlèiri

10

Coire nan
Clach

99

Lairig an Laoigh

10

04

05

06

07

08

09

Môine Bhealaidh

B
E
I
N
N

A

B
H
U
I
R
D

M

Dubh Lochan

A' Chioch
1179
South
Top
1177

Coire na
Ciche

98

continues on
PREVIOUS PAGE

Craig Derry
865

Coire an
Fhir Bhogha

© CROWN COPYRIGHT AND/OR DATABASE RIGHT. ALL RIGHTS RESERVED. LICENCE NUMBER 100025218.

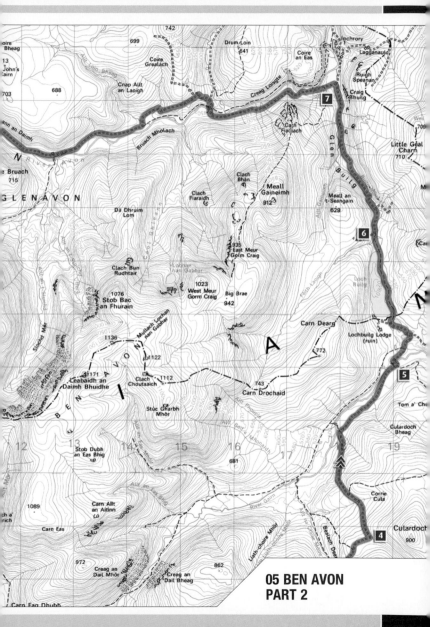

**05 BEN AVON
PART 2**

Directions – Ben Avon

1 From the car park at Linn of Dee follow the narrow road along the south side of the river into Braemar. Follow the A93 east for another 4.5km, crossing Invercauld Bridge.

2 Turn **L** into the Keiloch car park and continue towards Invercauld Castle.

3 Head north, following the signposts for *Loch Builg*. The tarmac soon gives way to stony Landrover track. The pines begin to thin out as you climb and, once through the trees, the track descends with fine views opening up to the east. The descent gives some respite before the loose stony climb to the highpoint of the ride at 730m on the western slopes of Cullardoch.

4 From the highpoint of the climb, the altitude you've just worked hard to gain is soon lost, dropping almost 400m down to follow the River Gairn.

5 Cross the river and climb to the main track for Glenbuilg Lodge. Turn **L** onto this track and then **R** after 400m to pick up the singletrack trail between the lochans at the end of Loch Builg. Follow this excellent, twisting singletrack to the northern end of the loch.

6 The track north of Loch Builg is quite boggy and can be indistinct in places. Aim for the obvious river valley to pick up the main Glen Builg track.

7 At the Linn of Avon turn **L** onto the track that crosses the river. Follow this good track west along Glen Avon to Faindouran bothy (optional overnight stop). From this track there are great views up the glen and to Ben Avon itself.

8 Beyond Faindouran, the hard work starts as the track deteriorates and becomes indistinct and very boggy in places. Prepare for plenty of pushing on this section.

9 At the Fords of Avon shelter, cross the river heading south into the Lairig an Laoigh. There are stepping stones, but these are usually under the water level. Pick up the singletrack trail which runs along the east side of Dubh Lochan.

10 The Lairig an Laoigh is the easier pass through the Cairngorms, and drovers preferred it for younger, less hardy cattle. For mountain bikers it's still tough as the singletrack gives way to boulders towards the top, and then peat. How much of this is rideable will depend on the ground conditions, but it soon improves to a good Landrover track.

11 Pick up the superb singletrack trail which runs down the west side of the Derry Burn, towards Derry Lodge.

12 Take the Landrover track into Glen Lui. After 3.2km, turn **R** and cross the river. 1.3km after the bridge take the final short section of singletrack back to the Linn of Dee car park.

Introduction

Glen Tilt is a long, winding glen, which follows the river as it flows south west from the wilderness that is the southern end of the Cairngorms towards the village of Blair Atholl. Ask any Scottish mountain biker their 'must do' routes, and this ride will certainly be near the top of the list. The loop makes a circuit of Beinn A'Ghlo, one of Scotland's most inaccessible Munros, and is truly epic. A tough, physical challenge with amazing scenery, big climbs, a real sense of remoteness and a flowing natural singletrack. If you're fit and well prepared, this is one of the best days you can have on your bike.

The Ride

From the Old Bridge of Tilt, the glen runs deep into the Forest of Atholl. The route passes remote farms and shooting lodges in the lower glen, before leaving civilisation behind and heading towards Beinn A'Ghlo. Branching off the main track, wonderful singletrack flows to the Bedford Bridge over the magnificent Falls of Tarf. Fording the river and scrabbling up a steep, loose climb leads to Fearlar Lodge, the most remote farmstead on the Scottish mainland. The sense of wilderness is particularly striking on the next section, where a fast and loose track drops to Daldhu. The final leg of the journey back to Blair Atholl takes in some amazing singletrack through the heather on the other side of Beinn A'Ghlo. This is a stunning ride, and one that every mountain biker should do.

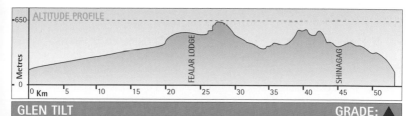

GLEN TILT

GRADE: ▲

DISTANCE: 54KM » **TOTAL ASCENT**: 1550M » **TIME**: 5–7 HOURS » **START/FINISH**: OLD BRIDGE OF TILT CAR PARK
START GRID REF: NN 875663 » **SATNAV**: BLAIR ATHOLL » **OS MAP**: LANDRANGER 43 » **CONTACT**: ATHOLL ESTATE
OFFICE TEL: 01796 481 355 » **PUB/CAFÉ**: ATHOLL ARMS HOTEL TEL: 01796 481 205

Directions – Glen Tilt

↻ From the car park at Old Bridge of Tilt, take the track that begins directly opposite the car park entrance. Follow this track, ignoring all junctions past the farms and houses at the southern end of the glen. Past Forest Lodge the track is not as well maintained, but good progress can still be made.

2 As the main track turns left and climbs steeply up the hill, take the rougher trail, which follows the river in the direction of the Falls of Tarf. Cross Tarf Water using the Bedford Bridge.

3 Approximately 400m after the Bedford Bridge, ford the river and climb the steep gravel track on the eastern bank leading to Fealar Lodge. **(Note: Fording this river can be very dangerous after heavy rain. Be prepared to turn back and save the remainder of this ride for another day if you are at all unsure. The track to Fealar Lodge can also be soft and is heavy going in places. Please get off and walk rather than churning up the peaty ground.)**

4 At Fealar Lodge pick up the well surfaced track which serves as the access road to the farm. This climbs gradually before beginning the 7km fast, rocky descent down to Daldhu.

5 At Daldhu, pass the first building and turn **R** onto the tarmac track, which comes as welcome relief after the battering of the descent. The tarmac soon deteriorates as the track runs alongside the Allt Glen Loch. A steep and rocky climb on the flank of Stac nam Bodach is a real leg breaker, but it's soon forgotten as superb, narrow singletrack cuts through the heather on the open descent to Shinagag.

6 From Shinagag, a good track leads west towards Loch Moraig. This reaches a single lane strip of tarmac at the loch, which drops steeply back to Old Bridge of Tilt.

continues on
NEXT PAGE

**06 GLEN TILT
PART 1**

© CROWN COPYRIGHT AND/OR DATABASE RIGHT. ALL RIGHTS RESERVED. LICENCE NUMBER 100025218.

© CROWN COPYRIGHT AND/OR DATABASE RIGHT. ALL RIGHTS RESERVED. LICENCE NUMBER 100025218.

continues on
PREVIOUS PAGE

**06 GLEN TILT
PART 2**

07 **Mount Keen** 55km

Introduction

Between April and July 1989, Paul Tattersall took a mountain bike to the summit of each of Scotland's 284 Munros. This feat has never been repeated, as it turned out that most Munro summits are not ideal for mountain biking. The bike had to be dismantled and ropes used on some occasions! Mount Keen however, is a bike friendly Munro. From Aboyne, an ancient trade route known as the Fungle Road takes you to Tarfside, where a good Landrover track runs right to the top of Mount Keen, 939m above sea level. The descent over the other side is superb. It begins by picking its way through boulders off the summit and funnels into a rocky singletrack, dropping almost 800m into Glen Tanar and back to Aboyne.

The Ride

From just outside Aboyne, the route follows the Fungle Road through the Forest of Birse to Birse Castle and then on to Tarfside. The surface of the first major ascent is generally good, giving a tough but rideable climb between the summits of Tampie and Mudlee Bracks. From Tarfside a heather-lined Landrover track climbs round the north side of the Hill of Rowan, past the Rowan Tower erected by the Earl of Dalhousie in the 19th century. From Invermark, the ascent of Mount Keen begins. It's gentle at first, passing Queen Victoria's Well in Glenmark before rearing up for the steep push up the mountain. The 360 degree summit panorama is worth savouring before the fantastic long descent back towards Aboyne.

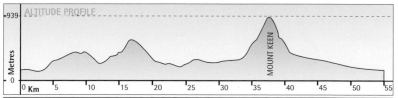

MOUNT KEEN   **GRADE:** ▲

DISTANCE: 55KM » **TOTAL ASCENT**: 1700M » **TIME**: 5–8 HOURS » **START/FINISH**: BRAELOINE VISITOR CENTRE CAR PARK **START GRID REF**: NO 480964 » **SATNAV**: AB34 5EU » **OS MAP**: LANDRANGER 44 » **CONTACT**: DALHOUSIE ESTATES TEL: 01356 624 566 » **CAFÉ**: CORNER HOUSE, ABOYNE TEL: 01339 886 427

© CROWN COPYRIGHT AND/OR DATABASE RIGHT. ALL RIGHTS RESERVED. LICENCE NUMBER 100025218.

continues on
NEXT PAGE

**07 MOUNT KEEN
PART 1**

continues on PREVIOUS PAGE

© CROWN COPYRIGHT AND/OR DATABASE RIGHT. ALL RIGHTS RESERVED. LICENCE NUMBER 100025218.

07 MOUNT KEEN
PART 2

1 From the car park at the Braeloine Visitor Centre car park, follow the minor road to the B976, heading east for another 2km after Bridge O'Ess.

2 Take the track signposted *Public footpath to Tarfside*. Climb the Fungle Road past the carved stone seat to the cottage known as The Guard. Carry on along the Fungle Road, emerging from the forest 1.5km after the cottage, before descending to the Water of Feugh just after Birse Castle.

3 From the river the next 5km are spent climbing to the highpoint of the Fungle Road, before all the work is rewarded with a 7km descent down to Tarfside. There are no facilities in Tarfside, so don't rely on picking up snacks in the village.

4 In Tarfside, cross the bridge and turn **R**, then immediately **L** onto a track that begins opposite the church. This old Landrover track is lined on each side and in the centre with heather and makes the climb around the Hill of Rowan relatively easy.

5 At Auchronie, join the tarmac for 600m before turning **R** onto a Landrover track, just before crossing the Water of Mark. Follow the glen past Queen Victoria's Well, where the steep push to the summit of Mount Keen begins.

6 Where the track splits, branch **R** to the summit. If visibility is poor, or you're feeling the distance, sticking to the track which traverses west of the summit reduces the total climbing by around 200m.

7 From the summit be careful in your line choice over the initial boulder fields. This is not the place to have an accident! The path narrows to a rock strewn singletrack, before opening out on the lower slopes.

8 Pick up the well surfaced Landrover track which runs down Glen Tanar. Usually the wind will be at your back on this section which makes for a high speed run down into the forest. Stay on the north side of the Water of Tanar, following the track to the minor road at Glen Tanar House and back to the car park.

Introduction

The Cairngorms mountain range is a must-ride destination for mountain bikers in the UK. There are hundreds of miles of trails, with something to suit every standard of rider. This epic, 200km circular tour uses historic cattle drovers' routes, winding singletrack and remote passes to travel around huge mountains carved by glaciers, through ancient woodlands of Scots Pine and around beautiful, clear lochs. The unique surroundings, amazing trails and real sense of wilderness make this an unforgettable MTB experience. The villages of Blair Atholl, Kingussie, Tomintoul and Braemar are perfectly placed to split the route into four days of magnificent wilderness riding, and provide facilities at the end of a tough day in the saddle.

The Ride

Starting the trip in Blair Atholl, quiet tarmac lanes act as a warm up before the Gaick Pass and Glen Tromie lead to the ruins of Ruthven Barracks and Kingussie. Some fabulous singletrack over the Moor of Feshie and through the ancient Scots Pines and silver birch of Rothiemurchus Forest brings you to Loch Morlich and the foot of the Ryvoan Pass. This old drovers' route climbs towards the Braes of Abernethy where some great woodland trails lead to Tomintoul, the highest village in the Highlands. From here the route heads south, through the giants of the Cairngorms to Braemar, on some wild and remote singletrack. Turning to the west the route follows the River Dee to Glen Tilt, the stunning steep-sided valley that meanders back to Blair Atholl.

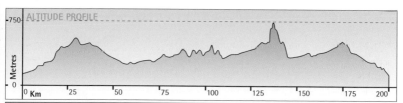

TOUR OF THE CAIRNGORMS   **GRADE:** ▲

DISTANCE: 200KM » **TOTAL ASCENT**: 4000M (APPROX) » **TIME**: 4 DAYS (4–8 HOURS PER DAY) » **START/FINISH**: BLAIR ATHOLL » **START GRID REF**: NN 871654 » **START SATNAV**: BLAIR ATHOLL » **OS MAPS**: LANDRANGER 35, 36, 42, 43
ESTATE CONTACTS: ATHOLL TEL: 01796 481 355. GAICK TEL: 01540 661 095. GLENTROMIE TEL: 01540 661 260
ROTHIEMURCHUS TEL: 01479 810 858. ABERNETHY (RSPB) TEL: 01479 821 409. GLENLIVET TEL: 01479 870 070
MAR LODGE TEL: 01339 741 433 » **ACCOMMODATION**: WWW.CAIRNGORMSHOSTELS.CO.UK WWW.VISITSCOTLAND.COM

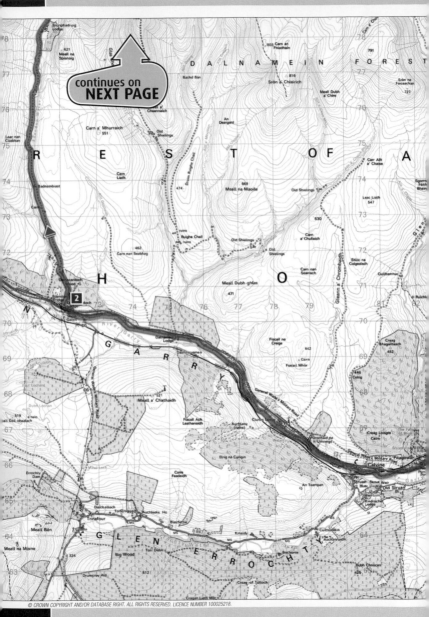

continues on
NEXT PAGE

2

© CROWN COPYRIGHT AND/OR DATABASE RIGHT. ALL RIGHTS RESERVED. LICENCE NUMBER 100025218.

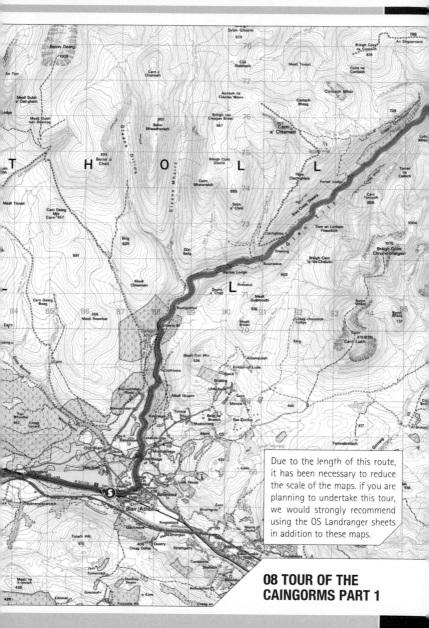

Due to the length of this route, it has been necessary to reduce the scale of the maps. if you are planning to undertake this tour, we would strongly recommend using the OS Landranger sheets in addition to these maps.

08 TOUR OF THE CAINGORMS PART 1

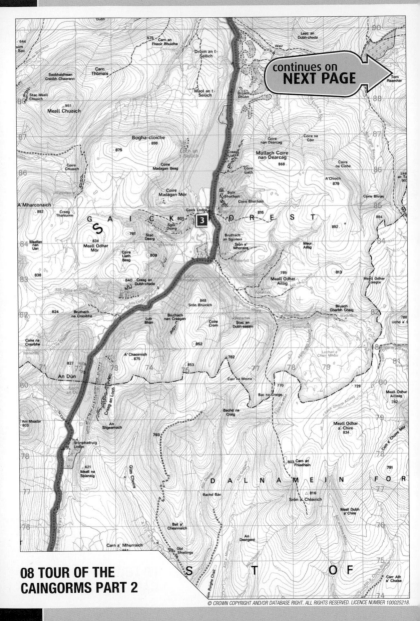

continues on **NEXT PAGE**

08 TOUR OF THE CAINGORMS PART 2

© CROWN COPYRIGHT AND/OR DATABASE RIGHT. ALL RIGHTS RESERVED. LICENCE NUMBER 100025218.

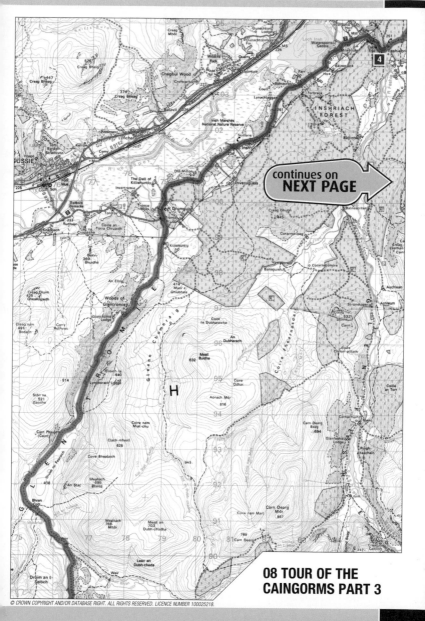

continues on
NEXT PAGE →

**08 TOUR OF THE
CAINGORMS PART 3**

© CROWN COPYRIGHT AND/OR DATABASE RIGHT. ALL RIGHTS RESERVED. LICENCE NUMBER 100025218.

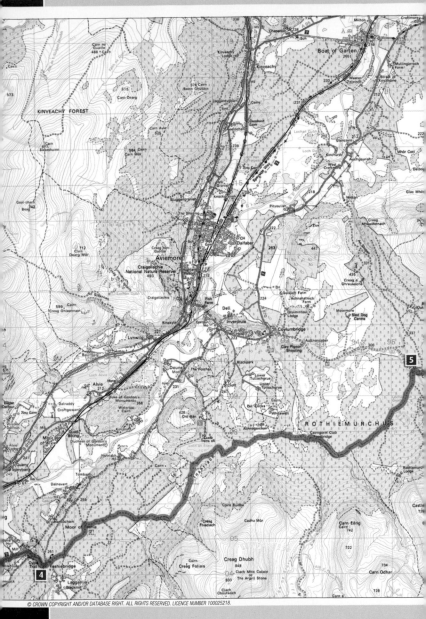

© CROWN COPYRIGHT AND/OR DATABASE RIGHT. ALL RIGHTS RESERVED. LICENCE NUMBER 100025218.

continues on
NEXT PAGE

**08 TOUR OF THE
CAINGORMS PART 4**

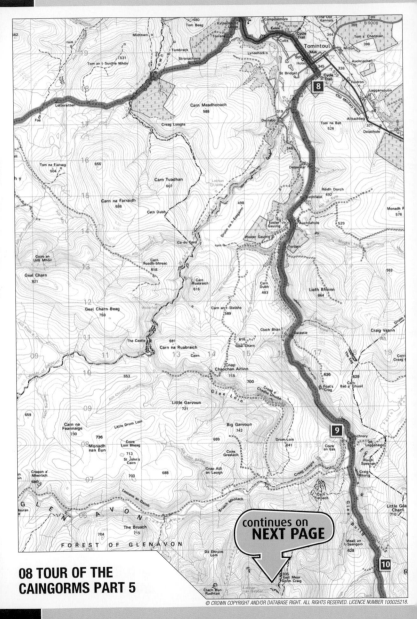

continues on
NEXT PAGE

**08 TOUR OF THE
CAINGORMS PART 5**

© CROWN COPYRIGHT AND/OR DATABASE RIGHT. ALL RIGHTS RESERVED. LICENCE NUMBER 100025218.

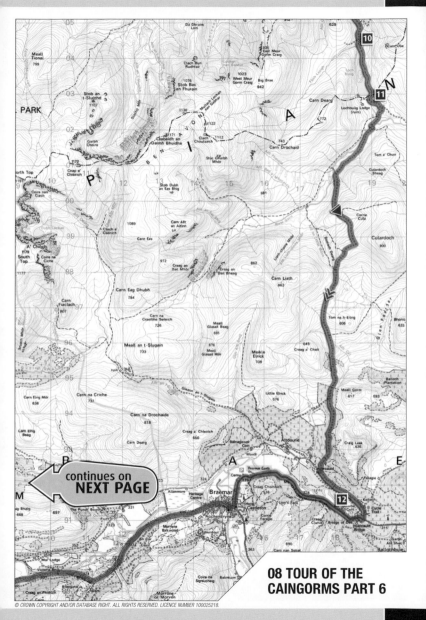

continues on
NEXT PAGE

**08 TOUR OF THE
CAIRNGORMS PART 6**

© CROWN COPYRIGHT AND/OR DATABASE RIGHT. ALL RIGHTS RESERVED. LICENCE NUMBER 100025218.

continues on
PAGE 161

08 TOUR OF THE CAINGORMS PART 7

© CROWN COPYRIGHT AND/OR DATABASE RIGHT. ALL RIGHTS RESERVED. LICENCE NUMBER 100025218.

Directions – Tour of the Cairngorms

◐➤ From Blair Atholl Railway Station follow the Sustrans Cycle Route north west out of the village for 16km.

2 Very carefully cross the A9 and climb north towards Sronphadruig Lodge and into the Gaick Pass. The singletrack along the edge of Loch an Duin is superb on this section, but there are several river crossings which may be impassable after heavy rain.

3 From Gaick Lodge, follow Glen Tromie to the minor road at Tromie Bridge. Turning left here will take you to Kingussie. Turn **R** to continue towards Feshiebridge.

4 At Feshiebridge, enter the forest and follow the forest tracks towards Drakes Bothy (Grid Ref: NH 884056). A wonderful section of rocky, rooty singletrack runs from the bothy to the southern end of Loch an Eilein. From the loch, follow the well-surfaced forest trails to the Cairngorm Club Footbridge and on to Loch Morlich.

5 Turn **R** and follow the road for 2.3km before branching off **L** towards Glenmore Lodge and the Ryvoan Pass. From Ryvoan Bothy, carry on over the summit of the pass, to the track junction 3.3km after the bothy.

6 Go **R** at this junction, crossing the River Nethy towards Loch a' Chnuic. Follow the narrow trail into Eag Mhor to Dorback Lodge. (The trail is not very well defined at this point, and is not marked on the map, but roughly follows the line of the stream, then goes through the trees and into Eag Mhor. The singletrack through the rocky cleft itself is real top stuff!)

7 From Dorback Lodge, follow Glen Brown to the main road into Tomintoul.

8 From Tomintoul take the minor road towards Delnabo, before branching off towards Queen Victoria Viewpoint. Follow the River Avon up the glen passing the magnificent Inchrory Lodge to the Linn of Avon.

9 At Linn of Avon, the main track swings round to the west and carries on up Glen Avon. Continue south into Glen Builg on the track that follows the east bank of the Builg Burn. The track becomes difficult to follow at the boggy north end of the Loch.

10 Pick up the great trail which runs alongside Loch Builg, before passing the beautiful lochans at its southern end and meeting the access road to the ruins of Lochbuilg Lodge.

11 Turn **L** onto this access road and then **R** after 400m, crossing the bridge over the River Gairn and climbing high onto the western flank of Cullardoch, before descending through the Bealach Dearg to Invercauld House on the outskirts of Braemar.

12 On reaching the main road turn **R** towards Braemar. From the centre of the village, 10 km of tarmac road leads to Linn of Dee, where the River Dee has cut a spectacular gorge in the rock.

13 From Linn of Dee take the track which follows the north bank of the River Dee towards White Bridge. Cross the bridge and follow the track towards the ruins of Bynack Lodge. You must cross the Geldie Burn to reach the lodge, and this is another river which may become impassable when in spate.

14 Follow the singletrack trail, which can be quite indistinct in places, over the watershed and down to the Falls of Tarf at the head of Glen Tilt by way of some superb technical riding. The singletrack trail clings to the steep sided valley above the river and those of a nervous disposition may prefer to get off and walk!

15 Cross the Bedford Bridge at the Falls, and follow the singletrack until it meets the main track through Glen Tilt. Follow the track down the glen. As you pass cottages and hunting lodges you'll know you're approaching civilisation at Blair Atholl again and the end of a memorable trip.

SECTION 4

Bonus section

Coast to Coast: Fort William to Montrose

Crossing Scotland from the Irish Sea to the North Sea has become one of the great mountain bike challenges and this route from Fort William on the west coast to Montrose on the east takes in some of the best trails Scotland has to offer. At almost 300km, this route has all the ingredients for the mountain bike trip of a lifetime.

Note: due to the length of this route, only overview mapping is provided. However, this route is relatively easy to plot onto the relevant OS sheets – which we'd highly recommend using regardless!

Bonus section
sponsored by **bike**magic.com

www.bikemagic.com

ROUTE CHECKING IN THE CAINGORMS

THE ASCENT OF MOUNT KEEN

Coast to Coast

Fort William to Montrose

290km

Introduction

Crossing Scotland from the Irish Sea to the North Sea has become one of the great mountain bike challenges. Riders from all over the world come to ride Scotland's excellent terrain and experience its hospitality and culture. This route, from Fort William on the west coast to Montrose on the east, takes in some of Scotland's finest trails. It shows off the country's varying landscape, from the jagged peaks of the west through rolling heather clad moors to the enormous flat-topped Cairngorm mountains and the fertile pastures of the east coast. At almost 300km, this route has all the ingredients for the MTB trip of a lifetime: great trails, wilderness adventure, fantastic mountain top views and winding valley singletrack.

The Ride

From the pier at Fort William the Great Glen Cycle Route is a gentle introduction to the trip, following the Caledonian Canal to the southern tip of Loch Ness. Climbing to almost 800m over the Corrieyarick Pass provides the first big challenge, before the Spey Valley leads towards Glen Feshie and the Cairngorms. This idyllic glen provides some amazingly remote singletrack riding, as it follows the glens to Braemar and Royal Deeside. Skirting Balmoral Castle, the holiday residence of the Royal family, the route climbs to the 939m summit of Mount Keen, Scotland's most easterly Munro. The Clash of Wirren provides the last section of stunning singletrack descent, before a final few miles of tarmac lead to the sandy beaches of Montrose and the North Sea.

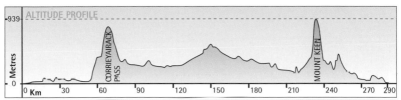

COAST TO COAST – FORT WILLIAM TO MONTROSE   GRADE: ▲

DISTANCE: 290KM » **TOTAL ASCENT**: 5500M (APPROX) » **TIME**: 5–7 DAYS (4–8 HOURS PER DAY) » **START**: FORT WILLIAM
START GRID REF: NN 104745 » **START SATNAV**: FORT WILLIAM » **FINISH**: MONTROSE » **FINISH GRID REF**: NO728581
FINISH SATNAV: MONTROSE » **OS MAPS**: LANDRANGER 34, 35, 41, 43, 44, 45, 54 » **ESTATE CONTACTS**: GLENSHERO
TEL: 01528 544 267. ROTHIEMURCHUS TEL: 01479 810 858. GLEN FESHIE TEL: 01540 651 880. MAR LODGE TEL: 01339 741 433.
BALMORAL TEL: 01339 742 534. GLEN TANAR TEL: 01339 886 451. MILLDEN & INVERMARK TEL: 01356 624 566
ACCOMMODATION: HOSTELS & BUNKHOUSES: WWW.HOSTEL-SCOTLAND.CO.UK WWW.SYHA.ORG.UK
B&BS & HOTELS: WWW.VISITSCOTLAND.COM

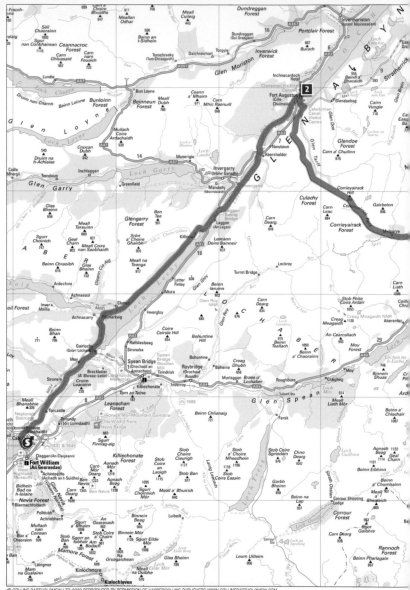

© COLLINS BARTHOLOMEW LTD 2009 REPRODUCED BY PERMISSION OF HARPERCOLLINS PUBLISHERS WWW.COLLINSBARTHOLOMEW.COM

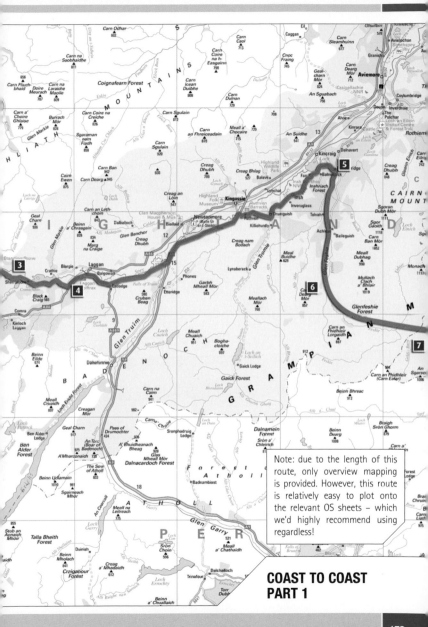

Note: due to the length of this route, only overview mapping is provided. However, this route is relatively easy to plot onto the relevant OS sheets – which we'd highly recommend using regardless!

COAST TO COAST PART 1

© COLLINS BARTHOLOMEW LTD 2009 REPRODUCED BY PERMISSION OF HARPERCOLLINS PUBLISHERS WWW.COLLINSBARTHOLOMEW.COM

**COAST TO COAST
PART 2**

Directions – Coast to Coast
Fort William to Montrose

➎ The pier at Fort William is a quiet starting point and allows for the obligatory west coast photo with Loch Linnhe in the background. Follow the *Great Glen Way* signposts past Inverlochy Castle and through the houses at Caol to the Caledonian Canal. The Great Glen Cycle Route is signposted the whole way to Fort Augustus. Crossing the canal at Laggan Locks and following the Great Glen Way avoids a major climb around Invergarry. This section may be busy with walkers.

2 From Fort Augustus, take Glendoe Road (B862) along the south bank of Loch Ness. After 1.5km turn **R** onto a narrow, tree lined road. Around 750m after the bridge over the River Tarff, turn **L** onto a track just before a farmhouse. Prepare yourself for the long and grinding ascent to the summit of the Corrieyarick Pass, almost 700m above. From the summit the descent has become washed out in places, and there are several sections of large scattered boulders to contend with before meeting the tarmac at Garva Bridge.

3 Take the short section of forest road, which leads off to the **R** just after passing the Spey Dam. This leads directly to Laggan Wolftrax, which has some of the most challenging purpose-built trails in the UK. It's well worth spending half a day riding the trails.

4 From Wolftrax follow the A86 for 2.8km, turn **R** onto the A889 and then take the minor road to the **L** at Catlodge. Follow this through the woods at Glentruim to pick up the Sustrans Cycle Route, parallel to the A9. This runs through Newtonmore and Kingussie, then past the ruins of Ruthven Barracks to Feshiebridge.

5 At Feshiebridge, turn **R** onto the track on the west side of the river, signposted *Right of Way to Deeside and Atholl by Glen Feshie*. Follow this track to meet up with the tarmac road which runs up the glen, with great views over the River Feshie.

6 Cross the river at the very rickety Carnachuin Bridge, continuing up the glen past Ruigh Aiteachain bothy. Shortly after the bothy, the hillside has been washed out and the track runs precariously along the steep slope above the river. Take extreme care on this section! After this tricky section things improve and some superb singletrack takes you further up the glen. The trail does make several crossings of the River Feshie, and these may be treacherous after heavy rain.

7 At the top of the glen take the bridge over the spectacular Eidart Falls, before taking the track which stays on the higher ground above the Geldie Burn. This section can be quite boggy, but soon improves to form a superb gravel singletrack, with plenty of rocks and water bars to test your bunnyhop skills.

8 Turn **L** where the singletrack meets the main Geldie Lodge access track and follow this over White Bridge to Linn of Dee. Take the minor road along the south side of the River Dee into Braemar, where there are pubs, shops and accommodation.

9 Follow the A93 east out of the village for 4.5km. Turn **R** and cross the Old Brig O'Dee. Follow the river past Connachat Cottage towards Balmoral Castle. If the Royals are in residence, you will most likely have to take the road towards Easter Balmoral. However you may be able to follow the trail along the riverbank on the north side of the castle. Either option brings you to the B976, which you follow to Ballater.

10 Cross the bridge and follow the A93 through centre of Ballater. Take Provost Craig Road to the **R**, just after the old station, and pick up the cycle lane that leads to Dinnet. This flat smooth path gives 10km of easy cycling. From Dinnet take the B9119 south and turn **L** onto the B976 at the junction. After 800m turn **R** towards Burnside on the Firmouth Road. Follow this past Home Farm and into Glen Tanar.

11 Cross the Water of Tanar and take the Mounth Road towards Mount Keen. The initial section is very steep, but just about rideable. Further up the track becomes extremely rocky and a sustained carry is needed to reach the summit. The 360 degree panorama from the summit definitely makes the climb worth it!

12 The descent from the summit of Mount Keen is fast, rocky and crosses dozens of stone water bars. Once into Glen Mark, the gradient eases and the track becomes smoother, passing Queen Victoria's Well towards the road in Glen Esk.

13 From the head of Glen Mark, either follow the tarmac towards Tarfside, or take the track which leads around the north side of the Hill of Rowan and descends into the village on some beautiful heather lined Landrover tracks.

14 Go through a gate and take the track which leads into the trees opposite a cottage. Cross the bridge over the River North Esk and climb through the fields to the saddle between Cowie Hill and Garlet. The track is not well defined on the ground and the grassy surface makes the climb hard work, but things are much easier on reaching Landrover track. The singletrack trail from the top of the Clash of Wirren down to Tillybardine Farm is superb. It's the last off-road section of the trip, so make sure you savour it!

15 Meeting the tarmac near Stonyford, all that remains is to follow the roads through Bridgend, Edzell, Keithock and Hillside towards the beach at Montrose.

16 At Hillside pick up the cycle route where it runs alongside the A937. Follow this into Montrose. It gets a little convoluted as it winds its way around the houses, but follow it until it runs along the edge of the golf course. At the junction with Traill Drive, opposite the golf clubhouse, turn **L** and follow the tarmac into the sand dunes. Make sure you take your east coast photo!

Please note

Due to the length of this route, only basic mapping is provided. However, this route is relatively easy to plot onto the relevant OS sheets – which we'd highly recommend regardless!

Alternatively, if you'd like to take on the challenge of the Coast to Coast but with the reassurance of a qualified guide, Scottish Mountain Bike Guides operate a 7 day tour – with full backup, meals, baggage transfers and mechanical support – allowing you to focus exclusively on some of the best mountain biking in the UK. **www.scottishmountainbikeguides.com**

Appendix

Listing every hotel, hostel, B&B, café and pub is a bit of a stretch for a guidebook that covers such a large area but here are a few bike shops, websites and other contacts that might come in handy.

Tourist Information Centres

General
T: 0845 22 55 121   www.visitscotland.com

Central & Southern Scotland
Dumfries
www.visitdumfriesandgalloway.co.uk
T: 01387 253 862

Edinburgh
www.edinburgh.org   T: 0845 225 5121

Glasgow
www.seeglasgow.com   T: 0141 204 4400

Newton Stewart
www.visitdumfriesandgalloway.co.uk
T: 01671 402 431

Peebles
www.scot-borders.co.uk   T: 01835 863 170

Stirling
www.visitscottishheartlands.org
T: 08707 200 620

Tyndrum
www.visitscottishheartlands.org
T: 08707 200 626

North West Scotland & Highlands
www.visithighlands.com

Broadford	T: 01845 2255 121
Drumnadrochit	T: 0845 2255 121
Fort Augustus	T: 01845 2255 121
Fort William	T: 01845 2255 121

North East Scotland & Cairngorms

Aberdeen	T: 01224 288 828
Aviemore	T: 0845 2255 121
www.visithighlands.com	
Ballater	T: 01339 755 306
Braemar	T: 01339 741 600
Kingussie	T: 0845 2255 121
www.visithighlands.com	
Pitlochry	T: 01796 472 215
www.perthshire.co.uk	

Hostels & Bunkhouses
Scottish Youth Hostels Association
www.syha.org.uk
T: 0870 155 3255 (reservations)
T: 01786 891 400 (general enquiries)

Scottish Independent Hostels
www.hostel-scotland.co.uk

Bed & Breakfast and Hotels
Visit Scotland   T: 0845 2255 121
http://cycling.visitscotland.com/accommodation
Details of accommodation providers which participate in Visit Scotland's 'Cyclists Welcome' scheme.

Bike Shops

Alpine Bikes   www.alpinebikes.com
7 shops throughout Scotland:

Aberdeen	T: 01224 211 455
Edinburgh	T: 0131 225 3286
Glasgow	T: 0141 353 2226
Innerleithen	T: 01896 830 880
Stirling	T: 01786 451 619
Glasgow Outdoor Experience	T: 0141 559 5450
Inverness Outdoor Experience	T: 01463 729 171

Edinburgh Bicycle Co-operative
www.edinburghbicycle.com

Aberdeen	T: 01224 632 994
Edinburgh	T: 0131 228 3565

The Hub – Glentress
T: 01721 721736   www.thehubintheforest.co.uk

Bothy Bikes – Inverdruie (by Aviemore)
T: 01479 810 111   www.bothybikes.co.uk

Fat Tread – Aviemore
T: 01479 812 019   www.fattreadbikes.co.uk

Off Beat Bikes – Fort William
T: 01397 704 008   www.offbeatbikes.co.uk

BaseCamp MTB – Laggan Wolftrax Trail Centre
T: 01528 544 786   www.basecampmtb.com

Escape Route – Pitlochry
T: 01796 473 859   www.escape-route.biz

Cycle Highlands – Ballater
T: 01339 755 864   www.cyclehighlands.com

Square Wheels – Strathpeffer
T: 01997 421 000   www.squarewheels.biz

Cycle Centre – Dumfries
T: 01387 259483   www.cycle-centre.com

Rik's Bike Shed – Drumlanrig Castle
T: 01848 330 080

Other contacts
www.outdooraccess-scotland.com
www.snh.org.uk/hillphones
www.mountainbothies.org.uk

Weather
www.mwis.org.uk
www.metoffice.gov.uk
www.midgeforecast.co.uk

The Author

Phil McKane has been addicted to riding mountain bikes since his fluorescent Emmelle was systematically rattled to pieces beneath him, around 1991. Since then he had dabbled in many aspects of mountain biking, from cross-country racing to wilderness touring. After completing his Masters degree in Sports Science, Phil set up **Scottish Mountain Bike Guides (www.scottishmountainbikeguides.com)**, operating mountain bike holidays and skills courses all over the country from the 7Stanes to the Western Isles.

The Photographer

Andy McCandlish has been riding mountain bikes since 1989 and he's been taking photographs almost as long. A freelance photographer and regular contributor to the cycling press – including **Mountain Bike Rider (MBR) Magazine** – Andy's stunning images are synonymous with mountain biking in Scotland. Andy can be contacted at **www.andymccandlish.com**

Vertebrate Publishing

Vertebrate Publishing is one of a new breed of independent publishers, dedicated to producing the very best outdoor leisure titles. We have critically acclaimed and bestselling titles covering a range of leisure activities, including; mountain biking, cycling, rock climbing, hillwalking and others. We are best known for our own titles such as *Lake District Mountain Biking* and *Dark Peak Mountain Biking*, which **BIKEmagic.com** said was *"far and away the best Peak guide we've come across".*

We also produce many leading outdoor titles for other publishers including the **Mountain Leader and Walking Group Leader Schemes (MLTUK)** and rock climbing guidebooks for the **British Mountaineering Council** and the **Fell and Rock Climbing Club**. For more information about **Vertebrate Publishing** please visit our website: **www.v-publishing.co.uk** or email us: **info@v-publishing.co.uk**

Other Publications

Mountain Biking Trail Centres – The Guide
Tom Fenton, Vertebrate Publishing
www.v-publishing.co.uk

VERTEBRATE PUBLISHING

MOUNTAIN BIKING GUIDEBOOKS

About the Great Outdoors

The great outdoors is not bottom bracket friendly; beautiful flowing singletrack can give way suddenly to scary rock gardens, hard climbs can appear right at the end of a ride and sheep will laugh at your attempts to clean your nemesis descent. Of course it's not all good news. You'll need a good bike to ride many of the routes in our set of mountain biking guides. You'll also need fuel, spare clothing, first aid skills, endurance, power, determination and plenty of nerve.

Bridleways litter our great outdoors. Our guides, written by local riders, reveal the secrets of their local area's best rides from 6 to 300km in length, including ideas for link-ups and night-riding options. Critically acclaimed, our comprehensive series of guides is the country's bestselling and most respected – purpose-built for the modern mountain biker.

The Guidebooks

Each guidebook features up to 28 rides, complete with comprehensive directions, specialist mapping and inspiring photography, all in a pocket-sized, portable format. Written by riders for riders, our guides are designed to maximise ride-ability and are full of useful local area information.

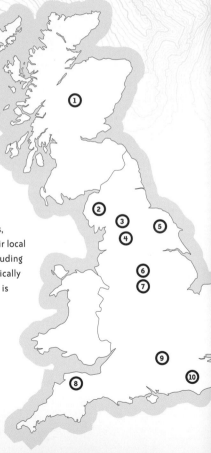

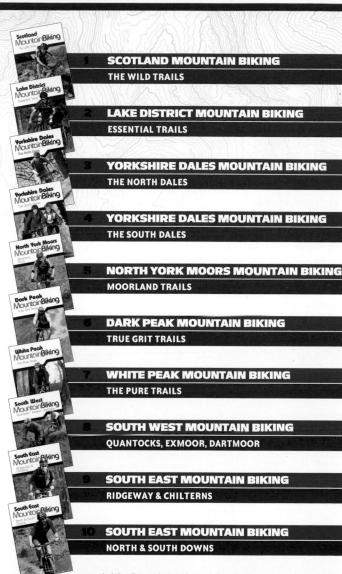

1 SCOTLAND MOUNTAIN BIKING
THE WILD TRAILS

2 LAKE DISTRICT MOUNTAIN BIKING
ESSENTIAL TRAILS

3 YORKSHIRE DALES MOUNTAIN BIKING
THE NORTH DALES

4 YORKSHIRE DALES MOUNTAIN BIKING
THE SOUTH DALES

5 NORTH YORK MOORS MOUNTAIN BIKING
MOORLAND TRAILS

6 DARK PEAK MOUNTAIN BIKING
TRUE GRIT TRAILS

7 WHITE PEAK MOUNTAIN BIKING
THE PURE TRAILS

8 SOUTH WEST MOUNTAIN BIKING
QUANTOCKS, EXMOOR, DARTMOOR

9 SOUTH EAST MOUNTAIN BIKING
RIDGEWAY & CHILTERNS

10 SOUTH EAST MOUNTAIN BIKING
NORTH & SOUTH DOWNS

Available from bikeshops, bookshops or direct from:
www.v-outdoor.co.uk

MOUNTAIN BIKING TRAIL CENTRES THE GUIDE

TOM FENTON

Mountain Biking Trail Centres – The Guide is the only comprehensive guide to the UK's network of purpose-built, off-road mountain biking trails, featuring thousands of kilometres of singletrack, cross country, downhill, freeride and bike park riding at 67 centres across England, Scotland and Wales.

Included are classics such as Dalby, Coed y Brenin and Glentress, lesser-known centres such as Balblair and Coed Trallwm, together with the latest developments including Whinlatter, Rossendale Adrenaline Gateway and many new trails at existing centres.

"This is without doubt the most comprehensive guide of its type available." MBR Magazine, Guidebook of the Month

"67 centres across England, Scotland and Wales are covered so if you're planning some trips, this is a must read before you load the car." BIKEmagic.com

"If you're planning an excursion to any trail centre, this book is a real gem. And if the pictures throughout the book don't inspire you to ride, we don't know what will." Bikeradar.com

"An absolute must for every committed trail rider in the country." planetFear.com

"This guide is essential for upping the quality of life of anyone with a mountain biking gene – just buy it." Adventure Travel Magazine

"If you ride bikes in the UK you simply can't afford to live without this book." Amazon Review

Available from all good book shops, bike shops and direct from www.v-outdoor.co.uk

VERTEBRATE PUBLISHING

Notes

07985 036944